The New York Times

Guide to
Management

Daniel J. Montgomery
Department of Communication
Florida State University

Jamie Murphy, Ph.D.
Visiting Fellow, Department of Information
Management and Marketing
University of Western Australia

South-Western College Publishing
Thomson Learning™

Australia • Canada • Denmark • Japan • Mexico • New Zealand • Philippines
Puerto Rico • Singapore • South Africa • Spain • United Kingdom • United States

The New York Times Guide to Management, by Daniel J. Montgomery & Jamie Murphy

Publisher: Dave Shaut
Acquisitions Editor: Pamela M. Person
Marketing Manager: Rob Bloom
Production Editor: Elizabeth A. Shipp
Media and Technology Editor: Kevin von Gillern
Media Production Editor: Robin K. Browning
Manufacturing Coordinator: Sandee Milewski
Internal Design: Joe Devine
Cover Design: Joe Devine
Copyeditor: Brian L. Massey
Production House: Trejo Production
Printer: Webcom

Printed in Canada
1 2 3 4 5 03 02 01 00

For more information contact South-Western College Publishing, 5101 Madison Road, Cincinnati, Ohio, 45227 or find us on the Internet at http://www.swcollege.com
For permission to use material from this text or product, contact us by
• **telephone: 1-800-730-2214**
• **fax: 1-800-730-2215**
• **web: http://www.thomsonrights.com**

Library of Congress Cataloging-in-Publication Data
Montgomery, Daniel J., 1944–
    The New York Times guide to management / Daniel J. Montgomery, Jamie Murphy.
        p. cm.
    ISBN 0-324-04157-8 (alk. paper)
        1. Management. I. Title: Guide to management. II. Murphy, James, 1950–
III. New York Times. IV. Title

HD31.M6184 2000
658--dc21   00-021221

This book is printed on acid-free paper.

P R E F A C E

The New York Times Guide to Management is designed for students, professors and business professionals—anyone interested in staying current in business today. A collection of the best management-related articles from the *New York Times*, this guide does more than inform: it also provides context for the effects of change on all aspects of business. Also included are articles from *CyberTimes*, the online-only technology section of the *New York Times on the Web*. Each article was selected for its relevance to today's business world.

In purchasing *The New York Times Guide to Management,* you are not only purchasing the contents between the covers, but also unlimited access, via password, to related *New York Times* articles. Current articles will be linked from the South-Western College Publishing/*New York Times* Web site (http://nytimes.swcollege.com) on an ongoing basis as news breaks.

This guide can be used formally in the classroom or informally for life-long learning. All articles are accompanied by exploratory exercises and probing questions developed by experts in the field. Previews provide context for each chapter of articles and link them to key management principles. This guide is divided into six sections organized to highlight critical factors in management today. This organization allows for easy integration into any management course.

Chapter 1: Management in a Changing Environment. Globalization multiplied by technology is rapidly changing today's managerial environment. Topics include: vertical integration, spin-offs, globalization, mergers, acquisitions, technology, and the perils of competition in today's environment.

Chapter 2: Managing Human Resources in a Changing Workplace. Litigation, labor problems and the question of how to train the leaders of tomorrow are but a few of the human resource problems that managers face. Topics include: demographics, diversity, workplace environment, temporary employees, training, free labor, litigious workplace, turnover and unions.

Chapter 3: The Role of Management Theory. This chapter explores the ever-changing role of theory, and its influences on management practices. Topics include: management theory, Peter Drucker, chaos theory, and complexity theory.

Chapter 4: Leadership. Leadership is more than formulas, rules and procedures. Personal qualities also influence a leader's success. Topics include: leaders, leadership, management styles, communication, decision making, organizational design, organizational change, managing conflict and teams.

Chapter 5: Management and the Role of Attitudes, Values and Ethics. Over the past several decades, managers have recognized that ethical behavior by management and employees can grow a business and make for a productive workplace. Topics include: corporate culture, crisis management, privacy, internal stakeholders, external stakeholders and values.

Chapter 6: Management and the Future. This closing chapter captures snapshots of trends that may influence tomorrow's workplace. Topics include: work ethic, entrepreneur, innovation, cross fertilization, changing employment trends, innovative work environment and today's manager.

PEDAGOGICAL FEATURES

Critical Thinking Questions challenge you to form your own opinion about current topics. These questions can be used to stimulate classroom discussion or as the basis for formal assignments.

Story-specific Questions highlight important points from each story.

Short Application Assignments work well as hands-on exercises for both classroom discussion and formal assignments. Most assignments should take no more than a few hours to complete. Typical assignments include developing presentations and writing brief memos, reports, executive summaries and articles for company newsletters.

Building Research Skills exercises allow you to expand upon what you have learned from the *New York Times'* articles and explore the unlimited resources available to enhance your understanding of current events. Typical assignments include presentations, writing essays and building Web pages.

ADDITIONAL ONLINE PEDAGOGY

Sample Exercises provide examples for you to follow in completing assignments.

Additional Readings link to more than 100 additional stories, categorized by chapter, for further research.

Featured Sections are in-depth collections of stories on specific topics such as Social Security, Outlook 2000, Retirement, the U.S. Budget, Welfare, and Is Microsoft a Monopoly.

Book Reviews cover about 80 computer and digital technology books reviewed by the *New York Times,* listed alphabetically by author and linked to the original review.

ACKNOWLEDGMENTS

Dr. Jamie Murphy is the inspiration for *The New York Times Guide to Management*. His efforts will benefit students throughout the world. He is a scholar and a gentleman. Thanks also to Dr. Brian L. Massey, Nanyang Technological University, Singapore, whose editorial contributions were invaluable. Drs. Murphy and Massey made this project a reality.

My thanks also extend to Melissa, John Paul, Ethan and Seth for their forbearance. I also want to thank my all-too-wonderful wife and my colleagues for their support.

C O N T E N T S

Management in a Changing Environment

PREVIEW

Today's managers face many challenges on top of the daily pressures of supervising a business, organization or department. The workplace keeps changing. Computer technology, mixed with Internet technology, is fueling two trends that already are changing today's business environment—globalization and mergers.

Nancy Hass reports on one reason for a wave of mergers in the entertainment industry: vertical integration. In "It's Synergy, Baby, Groovy! Yeah!" she explores how "so-called vertically integrated companies can spend the least money to make the biggest profit if all the divisions work together on every opportunity to market and merchandise every facet of a concept or character." In his report, "Tasty Morsels and Digestive Challenges for AT&T," Seth Schiesel uses analogies from the movie *Jaws* to explain mergers and acquisitions in the communications industry.

Globalization is also helping to consolidate the communication industry. But globalization means more than consolidation. For example, John Tagliabue's article "Will GE's Fresco Bring Good Things to Fiat?" investigates whether American-style management can revitalize an Italian company.

Finally, Amy Harmon's "With the Best Research and Intentions, a Game Maker Fails" illustrates the challenges faced by start-up companies in the technology industry. Money can buy research, ideas and top talent, but that may not suffice. Money buys you a ticket to play, but does not guarantee success.

It's Synergy, Baby. Groovy! Yeah!

By Nancy Hass

When "Austin Powers, International Man of Mystery" became a surprise hit back in May 1997, the executives at Time Warner did more than just congratulate the folks at their subsidiary, New Line Cinema.

They got to work.

For them, the spoof, starring Mike Myers as a foppish secret agent cryogenically frozen in the 1960s and thawed out in the present, had more than just laughs and an obvious sequel going for it ("Austin Powers II: The Spy Who Shagged Me" opens on June 11). With its goofy characters, accessible irony and catch phrases like "Shag-a-delic, baby," it provided an opportunity to demonstrate the raison d'être of the modern entertainment conglomerate: "synergy."

That concept, which has powered a wave of mergers and acquisitions in the last decade, is based on the theory that so-called vertically integrated companies can spend the least money to make the biggest profit if all the divisions work together on every opportunity to market and merchandise every facet of a concept or character.

And there is indeed a great deal of money to be made. Not just by Time Warner but by a slew of integrated behemoths like Disney, Polygram, Sony and Viacom. In the past, such add-ons as soundtrack albums, novelties, novelizations and foreign and television rights were mere bagatelles dwarfed by the domestic grosses of films themselves. Today, however, the equation has changed. And with advertising and promotion costs for movies soaring, the companies can make the most of the money they spend by selling everything— from keychains to theme park rides—at once.

"Licensing and the other revenue streams can now mean the difference between a $90 million base hit and a $150 million home run," said Ira Mayer, who owns *Licensing Letter*, an industry newsletter. Last year, nearly $16 billion of movie-related merchandise was sold.

For New Line, synergy at such a heady level is relatively new. For more than 30 years, the company was a scrappy independent studio. Then, in 1994, it was bought by Ted Turner and, two years later, absorbed by Time Warner as part of a merger.

At the time, critics fretted that New Line's quirkiness would be quashed by the corporate dictates of the parent company, that in the quest for synergy it would be turned into a mainstream studio like Warner Brothers.

Instead, by most accounts, New Line has retained its off-beat character—in addition to developing Austin Powers, it has released "Boogie Nights" and "American History X"—while growing downright comfortable with the resources of its parent company. "The opportunities presented by a movie like

'Austin Powers,'" said Michael Lynne, the president of New Line, "actually make you glad you're part of a big corporation."

Instead of giving up potential profits on toys and television rights, for instance, New Line can now keep the money all in the Time Warner family. Better still, the corporate hoopla means that a relatively modest movie—"The Spy Who Shagged Me" cost $30 million—has been transformed into an "event" film.

"There was a moment," recalled Mr. Lynne, "when we all realized that 'Austin Powers' was our 'Pink Panther,' that the first movie was just the beginning of the franchise." Bob Friedman, who oversees marketing and licensing for the company, puts it more bluntly: "To us, this 'Austin Powers' isn't a movie; it's a cable network."

And a board game. And a stuffed toy. And an animated series. And a potential hit for Madonna.

In fact, within weeks, Warner Brothers retail stores and Spenser Gifts stores across the country will roll out a plethora of merchandise from snazzy nightshirts to the Austin Powers Swedish Penis Enlarger ("the perfect gift for Dad on Father's Day!"). TBS and TNT, two cable networks owned by Time Warner, will feature wall-to-wall promotion of the movie. *Entertainment Weekly*, the glossy magazine owned by Time Warner, is set to have an Austin Powers cover.

Warner Records will release the soundtrack album, which includes a single, "Beautiful Stranger," by Madonna, whose label, Maverick Records, is also a Warner subsidiary. And by now, Warner Books has probably delivered to stores the first of its no doubt multiple printings of *The Austin Powers Encyclopedia*.

There's more. The home video, due out in the fall, will be sold by Time Warner's sales force; early next year there will be an animated series by HBO, a Time Warner subsidiary. "We are working on a relationship with the WB," said Mr. Friedman, referring to the youth-skewed broadcast network also owned by Time Warner. "They're perfect for us."

There may also be a theme park tie-in with Six Flags Great Adventure, which was sold recently by Time Warner but retains a licensing agreement with the company. "There's really no telling how far this thing can go and for how long," Mr. Lynne said.

But despite plucky New Line's smooth path to corporate nirvana, synergy is hardly an answer to all the industry's woes. After all, to make synergy work, studios need more than just a concept that has good merchandising potential.

"What people need to remember in the midst of all this," said Glen Brunman, the executive vice president of Sony Soundtrax, the leading maker of movie soundtrack albums, "is that none of this means anything unless there's a successful movie."

Even if a film is well-executed, too much synergy or too much at the wrong time can boomerang. Disney, widely considered a citadel of synergy, has learned some hard lessons of late. In the wake of "The Lion King" (1994), which raked in more than $1 billion in licensing revenue, the company promoted its 1997 animated movie "Hercules" with such fervor that it probably undercut the actual success of the film.

Not only did Disney saturate the market with merchandise from backpacks to sunglasses and wear kids out with television specials and parades, but it also aroused a backlash with its enthusiastic use of a flashing Hercules icon on promotions on ABC, the network Disney owns.

Among corporate entertainment executives, the "Hercules" campaign is now cited as an example of how too much synergy can cause "allegiance erosion." "What 'Hercules' taught everyone was that you can make a huge amount of money, but you have to be very careful about your timing and the appearance of over-commercialization," said a former Disney executive who is now a top marketer at a competing studio.

To that end, Disney's corporate synergy program last year for "Mulan" was much more low-key. While Michelle Kwan skated in a "Mulan"-inspired program on an ABC special, Disney made sure its merchandising was kept relatively elegant and upscale, in keeping with the nature of the animated musical about a young Chinese girl who disguises herself as a boy and joins the Imperial Army to bring honor to her family. Even the McDonald's Happy Meal tie-in didn't start until just before the film opened.

But restraint can be deadly as well. Sony, for example, waited to introduce its "Godzilla" merchandise until just before the film opened last summer, hoping to fuel demand—despite the fact that 40 percent of merchandise sales are typically made early on. When the movie was not the blockbuster it was built up to be (it made $136 million domestically; not bad, but not boffo), Sony probably wished it had put its action figures out early, to at least make up some of the slack for the film's disappointing box office.

Jay Roach, who directed both "Austin Powers" films but had previously worked only in independent films, spoke effusively about working with an entertainment conglomerate.

"There's a tendency to glamorize the freedom of working in the independent film world," said Mr. Roach. "But when I was working with individual backers, there were plenty of compromises. Everyone with money thought they knew how things should be done."

For Mr. Roach, Time Warner's muscle means one thing: the ability to grab more attention for his film. The sight of stuffed toy versions of Mr. Bigglesworth, the hairless cat character that appears in both "Austin Powers" films, may raise cries about rampant commercialism, but for Mr. Roach, it means the potential for a bigger box office return. And bigger box office will mean that he will be able to get not only more money for his next project, but more freedom.

"Sure, I was a little weirded out to see a life-sized doll of Verne Troyer," he said of a 32-inch-tall actor who plays a role in the sequel, "but it doesn't make me worry that I'm selling out my integrity. It makes me happy that the company has so much faith in the film. What talks in Hollywood is success. If that means that Time Warner makes money on the concept, I'm great with that, providing it means that I keep getting to make the movies I want to make."

Nor did he feel any corporate pressure to make his film more mainstream—the better to insure its marketing possibilities.

Although marketing executives were given copies of the shooting script and apprised of casting decisions, neither he nor Mr. Myers, a producer and co-writer of the film, were asked to change a single detail to conform to marketing or merchandising plans.

Nor did they participate in much of the planning for the firestorm of promotion. In a telephone interview late last month, Mr. Roach said it came as a surprise when a reporter told him that "Austin Powers" would anchor the Warner stores nationwide Father's Day promotion. "They do their thing and we do ours," he said, sounding a bit shocked.

But even true believers like Mr. Roach concede that soundtrack albums can be the troublemaker in a happily synergistic corporate family.

Once an afterthought released only when the movie was a musical or had a notably good instrumental score, soundtrack albums in the last few years have become one of the most lucrative spin-offs. The soundtrack for "Titanic," for example, made $31 million; "The Bodyguard" raked in $29 million.

But now that such albums are seen as an individual profit center and most movie studios are under the same corporate umbrellas as the recording companies, the possibility of conflict always lurks. Record companies have a slate of music makers to promote and a catalogue of songs to exploit. Not only may the filmmaker reject the artists signed by the parent company's record label; he may also want his studio to pay for outside performers and songs.

It's true that music companies sometimes push their own artists, said Mr. Brunman of Sony Soundtrax, but in the end, "the director always wins."

"Any company worth anything knows that you can't have the tail wagging the dog," he said. "The point of the whole exercise is the film."

Well, not always, especially with first-time filmmakers who are often hired guns with little leverage. Even for Mr. Roach, who is a hot property these days, the sequel soundtrack provided some tense moments.

He was extremely happy to take Warner's offer of Madonna's "Beautiful Stranger" for the movie's signature track, but in late April, just a few weeks before the film was set to open, there was some suggestion that he might be asked to include a few Warner artists who he didn't think were quite right, a sort of quid pro quo.

In the end Warner Music backed off, which was an enormous relief to Mr. Roach. "I know there are sometimes strings attached," he said, "but I have to say that I really wound up getting to do everything I wanted in making this film. If you ask me about corporate synergy, my personal experience is that everyone wins."

The New York Times, May 2, 1999

http://www.nytimes.com/library/film/050299film-sequel-synergy.html

CRITICAL THINKING QUESTIONS

1. For a company, what are the advantages and disadvantages of vertical integration? Do the advantages outweigh the disadvantages? Why, or why not?
2. Synergy often plays on the emotions of consumers, like the person who buys a sound track or a toy after seeing an emotional film in which the music or toy somehow was featured. Is this ethical? Should companies be allowed to exploit consumer emotions? What about instances where the consumer cannot afford the "add-on," but buys it anyway?
3. Although the article does not discuss it, what, in your opinion, might be the possible positive and negative consequences of synergy for the consumer?

STORY-SPECIFIC QUESTIONS

1. Synergy is synonymous with what term?
2. How is "New Line" an example of synergy?
3. What is the possible "downside" to synergy? Give an example.

SHORT APPLICATION ASSIGNMENTS

1. In teams or individually, answer the story-specific questions; keep your answers to 25–75 words for each question.
2. In teams of three to five persons, or as a whole class, discuss your responses to the critical thinking questions.
3. Prepare a one-page memo report (200–250 words) to your instructor in which you summarize this article. You will find a model one-page report on the Web site (nytimes.swcollege.com).
4. Write an executive summary (200–250 words). As an administrative assistant to a busy executive, you are expected to summarize selected articles and present important points. You will find a model executive summary on the Web site.
5. Summarize this article (100–125 words) for your company's newsletter. You will find a model newsletter article on the Web site.
6. Individually or in teams, generate a list of companies that have used the concept of synergy to enhance their profits. Give specific examples of the products they have marketed as "add-ons."

BUILDING RESEARCH SKILLS

1. Individually or in teams, use the World Wide Web and business literature (e.g., the *New York Times, Wall Street Journal*, or *Forbes* magazine) to research two companies that are using vertical integration, or "synergy." Your instructor may ask you to submit a three- to five-page essay, post a Web page or report your results in a five-minute presentation, along with a letter of transmittal explaining how the companies you have identified are vertically integrated.

2. Using at least three other references (e.g., books, research-journal articles, newspaper or magazine stories or credible Web sites), write an 800- to 1,000-word essay that addresses two of the earlier critical thinking questions. Assume that this essay will be used as an internal reference for a school or organization's crisis management plan.

3. Using at least three other references (e.g., books, research-journal articles, newspaper or magazine stories or credible Web sites), post an 800- to 1,000-word Web page that addresses at least two of the earlier critical thinking questions. Assume that this page will be posted in the policy section of a corporate intranet.

Tasty Morsels and Digestive Challenges for AT&T

By Seth Schiesel

Following the AT&T Corp. under C. Michael Armstrong has become an experience akin to watching one film sequel after another in the "Jaws" series.

Just when you thought that Armstrong, AT&T's chairman of 18 months, could not possibly bite off another big deal, he does just that, and the masses in the communications industry are sent fleeing to find ways to cope.

Last week's casualty may have been the Comcast Corp., the big cable television operator. Just when it looked as if AT&T had settled down to manage its own $31.8 billion acquisition of Tele-Communications Inc., the number two cable carrier, Armstrong swam into the middle of Comcast's pending $53 billion deal for the Mediaone Group and roiled the waters with an unsolicited bid for AT&T to buy Mediaone for $58 billion.

Mediaone executives have not yet publicly responded, but many analysts say that AT&T, with its superior financial power, will scare off Comcast and win Mediaone—if regulators allow it. That would make AT&T the nation's number one cable television company, in addition to the nation's number one long-distance telephone carrier.

But like a voracious shark that ends up with a bunch of old license plates in its belly, AT&T may have a tough time digesting everything it has tried to swallow. The main question for AT&T now is whether its appetite has exceeded its ability to integrate its businesses into the lean yet powerful communications machine that Armstrong wants AT&T to become.

As Armstrong propels AT&T headlong into the future he has envisioned, the company faces mounting challenges—not only of management and strategy, but also of regulation and technology.

Perhaps the most daunting management challenge for AT&T is the sheer breadth of Armstrong's strategic ambition. After John Zeglis, AT&T's president, was conspicuously absent during the company's Mediaone announcement last Thursday, several analysts wondered where he was.

It turned out he was in Japan. There, over the weekend, AT&T and British Telecommunications, AT&T's new international partner, announced a joint investment of more than $1.8 billion to acquire a 30 percent stake in Japan Telecom, a communications carrier backed by the main Japanese railroad company.

AT&T and British Telecommunications will also fold into Japan Telecom two of their existing Japanese ventures, with combined annual revenue of just more than $200 million.

The announcement's near simultaneity with the Mediaone bid was either impressive or unnerving, because it demonstrated Armstrong's comfort with juggling multiple deals. In fact, the Japan Telecom and Mediaone deals "are part of the same strategy," Zeglis said over the weekend. "We want to go end-to-end delivering services for our customers on our own architecture."

Despite AT&T's common goal of controlling its own architecture, or electronic infrastructure, there is a big difference between these two deals. AT&T's overseas ventures are aimed at serving big-ticket multinational corporate clients, while the company's cable television expansion is aimed at serving everyday residential consumers. It is the company's hunger for residential customers that best explains AT&T's seeming feeding frenzy.

It is clear by now that AT&T is terrified of the prospect of at least one of the local Bell phone companies, probably Bell Atlantic, being poised to win regulatory approval to enter AT&T's core long-distance business this year.

By way of a harbinger, AT&T is well aware of what happened in Connecticut after the Southern New England Telecommunications Corp., which did not need special approval, began offering long-distance service to Southern New England's local phone customers. Large numbers of Connecticut customers dropped long-distance service from AT&T, among others, to take a single package of local and long distance from SNET.

AT&T's strategic planners hate to contemplate the millions of local phone customers who might drop AT&T phone service once Bell Atlantic is freed to offer long-distance service to customers along the Eastern Seaboard, or even just in New York. It is a much bigger worry for AT&T than for its principal long-distance rivals, MCI Worldcom and Sprint, because AT&T derives a much higher proportion of its long-distance revenue from residential consumers than do MCI and Sprint.

Armstrong has decided that the solution is to counterattack the Bells by taking the war to a new front—off the conventional local telephone network and onto cable TV systems. Through those cable lines, AT&T intends to offer local and long-distance calling, as well as Internet service.

It will probably take a few years to determine whether that strategy is visionary or foolhardy. AT&T would like to offer its cable-based services using a variant of Internet technology. Because this is a largely experimental approach, it poses large technical challenges. It may, however, prove easier in Mediaone territories than in TCI areas, because Mediaone's network is generally more technically advanced. That is why AT&T is willing to pay more for Mediaone than it did for TCI, even though TCI has more customers.

The cable strategy also raises management questions. AT&T is well practiced in telephone-network technology, but linking so much of its future to cable television networks means the company needs to rely on experts from outside the AT&T tradition. Foremost among them is Leo Hindery, the former number two executive at TCI who now runs AT&T's cable operation—but who is still largely unfamiliar with AT&T and its culture in offering telephone service. The same could be said for the highly respected Amos B. Hostetter, Mediaone's largest shareholder, who AT&T has said will become chairman of its cable and Internet unit if its Mediaone bid succeeds.

But before Hostetter can come aboard, AT&T must not only fend off Comcast, but also convince Federal regulators that a combined AT&T-TCI-Mediaone would not wield disproportionate power in the cable television industry. Under Federal Communications Commission ownership rules, no single entity can control cable systems that together are available to more than 35 percent of the nation's households. But those rules have been suspended pending a review by the FCC.

There are financial imponderables. AT&T—with backing from Chase Manhattan Bank and Goldman, Sachs & Co.—seems set to raise $30 billion in cash to support its Mediaone bid. But Standard & Poor's, the credit-rating agency, said on Friday that it was considering downgrading AT&T's debt to reflect the big financial burden the company will take on if it acquires Mediaone.

The stakes for Armstrong, not to mention AT&T, are high. They keep escalating. If the cable strategy works well, he will become known as one of the most visionary and dynamic executives of his day. If it does not, business history might one day recall him as a former IBM executive who was passed over for the top job at that company and who, later, when given the chance to run AT&T, tried to prove too much.

For now, at least, dynamic seems to be winning. Armstrong, presumably, is looking for his next "Jaws" sequel.

The New York Times, April 26, 1999
http://www.nytimes.com/library/tech/99/04/biztech/articles/26att.html

CRITICAL THINKING QUESTIONS

1. To acquire or not, "that is the question." What are the potential risks and possible benefits faced by corporations that are considering an acquisition?
2. What challenges do managers face when acquiring an organization?
3. When, if at all, should the government restrict corporate acquisitions?

STORY-SPECIFIC QUESTIONS

1. What is the rationale behind C. Michael Armstrong's acquisitions?
2. What is the single biggest challenge that Armstrong's "strategic ambition" poses for AT&T?
3. Why is Armstrong waging his war against the Bells on a "new front?" What is Armstrong's rationale?

SHORT APPLICATION ASSIGNMENTS

1. In teams or individually, answer the story-specific questions; keep your answers to 25–75 words for each question.
2. In teams of three to five persons, or as a whole class, discuss your responses to the critical thinking questions.
3. Prepare a one-page memo report (200–250 words) to your instructor in which you summarize this article. You will find a model one-page report on the Web site (nytimes.swcollege.com).
4. Write an executive summary (200–250 words). As an administrative assistant to a busy executive, you are expected to summarize selected articles and present important points. You will find a model executive summary on the Web site.
5. Summarize this article (100–125 words) for your company's newsletter. You will find a model newsletter article on the Web site.
6. Individually or in teams, assume that you are a part of AT&T's management team. Armstrong has asked you to critique his management strategy. Develop a proposal (250–500 words) that highlights the pros and cons of Armstrong's vision of the future and his strategy for achieving it.

BUILDING RESEARCH SKILLS

1. Individually or in teams, research any other acquisitions that AT&T has made since this story was written. What, if any, rulings have the United States or other governments made regarding AT&T's acquisitions since this story was written? Your instructor may ask you to submit a three- to five-page essay, post a Web page or report your results in a five-minute presentation, along with a letter of transmittal explaining your results.
2. Using at least three other references (e.g., books, research-journal articles, newspaper or magazine stories or credible Web sites), post an 800- to 1,000-word Web page that addresses two of the earlier critical thinking questions. Assume that your Web page will be used as an internal reference for a corporation's intranet.
3. Using at least three other references (e.g., books, research-journal articles, newspaper or magazine stories or credible Web sites), write an 800- to 1,000-word essay that addresses two of the earlier critical thinking questions. Assume that your essay will be used as an internal reference for a corporation's business plan.

Will GE's Fresco Bring Good Things to Fiat?

By John Tagliabue

TURIN, Italy—For most of Fiat's 132,000 Italian employees, breakfast usually consists of little more than an espresso and a newspaper. But on a recent morning, Paolo Fresco sat ramrod straight in a dining room of Fiat's executive suite and, in vaguely accented English, ordered "scrambled eggs, very soft, and a side order of bacon—very, very crisp."

Fresco, 66, a large athletic man with silvery hair, was born in Italy and holds an Italian passport. Fourteen months ago, he became chairman of Fiat SpA, the industrial giant that is one of Italy's biggest corporations. He is, in short, as Italian as they come.

But as his culinary preferences reflect, Fresco's fabric goes well beyond his heritage. For nearly four decades, he worked for General Electric, a darling of American investors, climbing the corporate ladder to become vice chairman under John F. Welch Jr. before retiring from the company last year.

Now he is bringing some of his—and perhaps Jack Welch's—American ways to the task of revitalizing Fiat.

Fresco is not the first of Welch's disciples to carry GE's genetic code elsewhere. In 1991, Lawrence A. Bossidy left the company to lead a turnaround at Allied Signal; the next year, Glen H. Hiner departed to test his mettle at Owens Corning.

What makes Fresco's story intriguing is his effort to take a chapter from the Welch book of American-style management to Italy, a land of cosseted industries and traditions like lifetime employment.

The tenets of GE management include being number one or number two in a business, or getting out of it; picking managers that can motivate people and make them work as a team; encouraging communication; thinking long-term and strategically, instead of just tactically; building shareholder value.

"The company that doesn't change doesn't survive," Fresco said, downing his bacon and eggs while quoting Welch, then washing it all down with a cup of American coffee topped with a dollop of cream.

Americans think of Fiat as an auto company, but its empire extends far beyond cars, to farm equipment, insurance and even a daily newspaper here, *La Stampa*. This year, for the first time, cars will account for less than half of Fiat's roughly $50 billion in revenue, and it is Fresco's charge to run Fiat as a modern conglomerate, like GE.

That could entail fundamental change for a company celebrating its 100th birthday. Fiat's car division is losing ground in global rankings.

Producing fewer than three million cars a year, it lacks the scale of General

Motors, Ford Motor or Toyota Motor and faces powerful new alliances like the DaimlerChrysler combination and the Renault's tie-up with Nissan Motor. Losses in the last four quarters underscore Fiat's weakness.

And so Fresco, a lawyer by training, may end up presiding over the company's departure from the car business, through a merger or sale.

"We can continue to be alone," he said. But, he added, "that doesn't mean you turn down an offer if it comes across."

His comment echoes the views of Gianni Agnelli, Fiat's chief shareholder and honorary chairman. Agnelli's grandfather founded the company and has known Fresco since the early 1960s, when Fresco was hired by an Italian GE unit of which Fiat was part-owner, to set up a legal department.

"Today, Fiat cars is in a position to proceed on its own, but it neither can nor wants to do that forever," Agnelli, 78, told a shareholders meeting in July. "It is destined to find some form of alliance. Which and when, I do not now know. I do know, however, that it is equipping itself."

One Fiat executive with regular access to Fresco is more blunt: "Fresco's role is to get the bride ready for a suitor."

The chairman has wasted no time putting to work for Fiat the deal-making skills that he honed at GE.

In May, he rushed to Racine, Wisconsin, to sign a $4.3 billion deal to buy the Case Corp., the heavy-equipment manufacturer that he is combining with Fiat's New Holland unit. The size of the merged company will rival that of Deere & Co. in farm machinery and that of Caterpillar and Komatsu in construction equipment.

Two months earlier, he agreed to pay $350 million to acquire Progressive Tool and Industries of Southfield, Michigan, for Fiat's Comau unit, now among the world leaders in automobile manufacturing systems. Before that, Comau acquired control of Renault Automation, which also makes auto factory equipment.

And there have been other deals. Last year, for instance, Fiat and Renault agreed to merge their foundry units, which cast heavy metal parts, and their bus-building businesses. At the same time, Teksid, Fiat's foundry company, struck a deal with the Eaton Corp. of Cleveland to make cylinder head systems, following a trend for components manufacturers to produce large subassemblies for cars and trucks. This summer, Fiat agreed with Mitsubishi to develop a sport utility vehicle for sale in Europe.

But Fresco's most daring bid failed. Earlier this year, he and Paolo Cantarella, Fiat's chief executive, offered $15 billion to acquire Volvo, whose car, bus and truck operations Fresco says were a perfect fit for Fiat's similar businesses. Volvo's unwillingness to sell the entire operation—and a $6.5 billion counterbid by Ford for Volvo's car business alone—thwarted the plan. The episode has been the lone major setback for Fiat shareholders since markets shook off Russia's financial problems last fall.

Within the company, the product cycle was of no help: the original Punto compact car—Fiat's entry, in the early '90s, into the biggest and most lucrative market segment in Europe, and Europe's best-selling car in 1997 and 1998—was reaching the end of its shelf life. And Fiat's top-of-the-line Alfa Romeo and Lancia models were also reaching the end of their cycles.

But Fresco says the car division is now on the right track. In July, Fiat introduced a redesigned Punto. And the company is reviving the sporty Alfa Romeo brand with two stylish models, the 156 and 166, and the big-car Lancia brand with a new model called the Lybra.

Fresco also defends Fiat's strategy of focusing on emerging markets. "Those are the only markets where you can expect growth," he said, adding, "I believe our specialization in small cars, where we have competence, puts us in an attractive strategic position."

Fiat, he said, will continue to hunt aggressively for partnerships with other car and component makers and will work on cutting costs in production and distribution, where it has already begun to weed out dealerships. By the last quarter of the year, he vowed, Fiat cars will be back in the black.

With nine years to go before he reaches Fiat's mandatory retirement age, Fresco may find that his success will depend at least in part on his ability to get the company's workforce to match his energy and focus on results.

Traditionally, Fiat's ability to reward merit has been bogged down by internal rules, often demanded by powerful labor unions, requiring carefully staggered pay raises and at least two years between promotions, said Nevio Di Giusto, senior vice president for development.

"If Fiat had a weakness, we were accused of treating people indifferently of their performance," he said.

That must change, Di Giusto said—and managers must learn to bring weaknesses to light mercilessly, rather than trying to conceal them. "The world's getting more open, and this has to find expression in Fiat," he said.

Already, Fresco has proposed stock options for Fiat's top 700 executives, and he wants to spread the reward system down to middle management. His own compensation and that of Cantarella includes stock options and is also linked directly to the performance of Fiat's stock, a rarity not only in Italy but in the United States as well.

His success may also depend on his ability to identify new areas of growth. In his Welch-style search, he is stressing services, including financial products.

"The idea is not so much to give some new widget to the customer, but total solutions," he said. "And in the car business, that means selling peace of mind." In one planned solution, he said, if a customer's car broke down, Fiat would supply a new one; in commercial vehicles, a total solution could mean expanding the leasing business. A plus is that the required investment is minimal, compared with changing manufacturing lines.

To prepare for the growth of the company's financial services businesses,

Fresco has recast the financial management, appointing Damien Clermont, a Frenchman who previously was senior vice president for management control at Fiat, as chief financial officer.

Here, too, parallels with GE are inescapable. "Welch ran a top team, very informally, with lots of interaction," Tichy said. "Everyone is expected to add value. It's not a one-man show."

Indeed, Fresco bristles at those who refer to a Fresco era at Fiat. On a recent Sunday, he watched television aboard his yacht as Fiat's fabled Ferrari racing team finished one-two in the German Formula One Grand Prix. Mika Salo, a Ferrari driver, moved aside to let Eddie Irvine, another Ferrari driver, win the race, raising Ferrari's overall standing in the season's ranking under a complex tallying system.

"This was not just one man; it was a team," Fresco exulted. "And that's the way we want to be—a team. We want to win."

The New York Times, September 12, 1999
http://www.nytimes.com/library/world/europe/091299fiat-fresco.html

CRITICAL THINKING QUESTIONS

1. Usually, when management instigates change there is resistance. What steps can management take to make change more palatable for employees?
2. Instituting and guiding organizational change poses a number of challenges for managers, including management and public relations problems. If you were to develop a strategy for bringing about change at Fiat with a minimum of negative side-effects, would you follow the Paolo Fresco strategy or pursue an alternative? Why?
3. What considerations, if any, should Fresco make before imposing American-style management practices on Fiat? Why?

STORY-SPECIFIC QUESTIONS

1. What are two General Electric management strategies or philosophies that Paolo Fresco will bring to Fiat?
2. Why is Fiat interested in developing partnerships?
3. In his attempt to instill such work ethics as excellence and pay for performance, what are two challenges that Fresco faces?

SHORT APPLICATION ASSIGNMENTS

1. In teams or individually, answer the story-specific questions; keep your answers to 25–75 words for each question.
2. In teams of three to five persons, or as a whole class, discuss your responses to the critical thinking questions.

3. Prepare a one-page memo report (200–250 words) to your instructor in which you summarize this article. You will find a model one-page report on the Web site (nytimes.swcollege.com).
4. Write an executive summary (200–250 words). As an administrative assistant to a busy executive, you are expected to summarize selected articles and present important points. You will find a model executive summary on the Web site.
5. Summarize this article (100–125 words) for your company's newsletter. You will find a model newsletter article on the Web site.
6. Individually or in teams, research General Electric. What are the management practices that make General Electric successful? Prepare a report (250–500 words) outlining your answer.

BUILDING RESEARCH SKILLS

1. Find at least one other company that has brought in a CEO (chief executive officer) from another sector of the marketplace. Has the move been successful? Why, or why not? Your instructor may ask you to submit a three- to five-page essay, post a Web page or report your results in a five-minute presentation, along with a letter of transmittal explaining your summary.
2. Using at least three other references (e.g., books, research-journal articles, newspaper or magazine stories or credible Web sites), post an 800- to 1,000-word Web page that addresses two of the earlier critical thinking questions. Assume that your Web page will be used as an internal reference for a corporation's intranet.
3. Using at least three other references (e.g., books, research-journal articles, newspaper or magazine stories or credible Web sites), write an 800- to 1,000-word essay that addresses two of the earlier critical thinking questions. Assume that your essay will be used as an internal reference for a corporation's business plan.
4. The article illustrates what happens when two cultures clash. Write an essay (500–1,000 words) that explains how Fresco should address these cultural differences. Examples include treating employees the same regardless of their performance, and the union rules and regulations that require "two years between promotions."

With the Best Research and Intentions, a Game Maker Fails

By Amy Harmon

SAN FRANCISCO—Paper dolls still cling to the walls of the deserted loft where Purple Moon LLC sought and failed to make a viable business out of computer games for girls—titles that in contrast to current top-sellers, were not about eye shadow selection, nail-polish tricks or adventures around the pressing question, "Where's Ken?"

The cut-outs, representing girls of different colors and sizes kicking soccer balls and holding hands, reflect the company's goal of creating a Barbie alternative that would inspire preteen-age girls to embrace the personal computer.

On Friday, Purple Moon's chief executive and sole remaining employee, Nancy Deyo, looked as forlorn as the abandoned dolls as workers arrived to cart away the last copying machine.

The day before, the deal she had been struggling to close when the company ran out of money last month went through—albeit in a much-altered form. In a move that seemed bittersweet if financially pragmatic, Barbie's corporate parent, Mattel Inc., announced plans to purchase Purple Moon's assets.

"I think Purple Moon made a difference for girls, and I'm proud to have done that," Ms. Deyo said.

In some ways, the story of Purple Moon mirrors that of hundreds of Silicon Valley start-ups that spend millions of dollars each year only to fail before they can change the world and make huge returns for their owners in an initial public offering.

Small and unknown, Purple Moon faced an unforgiving battle for shelf space with Mattel, which had 6 of the top 10 girls' titles last year—all Barbie themes—according to PC Data, a market research firm. The four others featured Madeline, French heroine of the much-loved children's books, in titles published by the Learning Company, which Mattel is also acquiring.

That Mattel was eager to scoop up Purple Moon's products—for an undisclosed sum—helps refute assertions that the small company's failure confirms that girls just want to play Barbie Magic Hair Styler.

Mattel said it planned new titles based on Rockett, Purple Moon's spunky heroine, who favors spiky orange bangs and such issues as whether to join the popular clique at school. The Los Angeles-based Mattel also was impressed by the popularity of Purple Moon's World Wide Web site, which has 250,000 registered users.

"We agree with the research they've done to show that there is a different way for girls to play with computers," said David Haddad, president of Mattel Media.

But at a time when electronic commerce and Internet portal sites are the darlings of Wall Street, Purple Moon's business failure invites scrutiny of the steps and missteps that led to the dismissal of the company's 40 employees—at more than 80 percent women, the reverse of Silicon Valley's typical gender ratio—on February 18.

The brainchild of Brenda Laurel, a game designer whose credits include Atari in the early 1980s, Purple Moon evolved from her work at Interval Research Corp., which was financed by Microsoft's co-founder Paul Allen. Over four years, Ms. Laurel interviewed 1,000 girls in researching how to apply the principles of their play to computer games.

By the time the company was spun off, underwritten by Interval and Allen's Vulcan Ventures, it seemed clear to Ms. Laurel that girls were not turned off by the violence in boys' games so much as they found dying and starting over again tedious. Boys liked overt competition; girls liked covert competition. Boys liked superheroes and fantastical adventures; girls liked challenges they could recognize in their lives.

"Brenda thought it through better than anyone else, and it still failed," said Henry Jenkins, director of comparative media studies at the Massachusetts Institute of Technology. Jenkins, an editor of *From Barbie to Mortal Kombat*, an anthology on gender and computer games published by MIT Press, added, "That's very frustrating and very worrisome."

The company used radical game features like emotional navigation and relationship hierarchies to carve out a space for girls in a market that had long been aimed at boys.

The approach attracted plenty of media attention. "A ROM of Their Own," a *Time* magazine headline proclaimed before Purple Moon introduced its first products.

Spending was not spared. Early on, at a company retreat, the development team role-played the proposed game characters to try to understand their inner lives. In Christmas seasons, Purple Moon bought television advertising.

The exhaustive research in which the company had its roots continued with 25 additional studies. One, an ethnographic study of girls' interest in sports, led to a product line featuring soccer, which Mattel appears least interested in continuing. Some critics argue that Purple Moon's strong focus on research proved no substitute for more nimble business strategies.

It is a criticism that Ms. Laurel acknowledged in her keynote address to the Computer Game Developer's Conference in San Jose, California, on Thursday.

"I promised to talk to you about some approaches to research and design that will help us grow both our audiences and our ideas," she said, addressing the pony-tails-and-sneakers crowd in a green print dress, horn-rimmed glasses and sensible shoes. "But since Purple Moon did not make it to the big IPO or a lavish acquisition that made everybody rich, it would be understandable for you to conclude that the methods I'm advocating don't necessarily work."

Afterward, Ms. Laurel—who said she had spent the last few weeks answering e-mail from parents and girls distraught at the news that Purple Moon was no more—blamed tough competition, bad timing and perhaps unrealistic expectations by her private investors.

"There was a fundamental disagreement over how the company should be valued," said Ms. Laurel, a board member and the company's vice president for design.

Purple Moon had been seeking a buyer since the board decided last fall that a public stock offering was out of reach, she said. Even so, she said she was surprised when the investors, including Institutional Venture Partners of Menlo Park, California, and the investment banker Allen & Co. gave up, in part because she believed that the deal being discussed with Mattel could be worked out.

Both Ms. Laurel and Ms. Deyo now say that they should have considered exit strategies sooner. But others close to the company criticized Ms. Laurel's grasp of business.

David Liddle, chairman of both Interval and Purple Moon, said: "Did Interval make a lot of money from this? No, I was disappointed. We had hoped the company would be big and successful on its own."

Whatever its business failings, Ms. Laurel suggests, Purple Moon may have helped broaden girls' attitudes toward technology and the software industry's attitude about girls and technology.

According to PC Data, the market for girls' CD-ROM titles grew 38 percent last year.

Mattel says it will soon offer a line of interactive products that includes Barbie, a series based on American girls in different historical periods, and Rockett.

"I'm proud to have created value," Ms. Laurel said. "It would have been nice to have created enough value to send my kids to college. But I certainly got an education."

The New York Times, March 22, 1999
http://www.nytimes.com/library/tech/99/03/biztech/articles/22moon.html

CRITICAL THINKING QUESTIONS

1. This story illustrates several of the problems faced by new entrepreneurs. What are some of these problems? Are there other problems?
2. Do the interests of young men and women in computer games differ? Why would a young woman prefer one game and a young man another? Or, is the gender difference non-existent or exaggerated?
3. What are the unique problems and opportunities posed by the trend of "bigger is better?" Specifically, what problems does it pose for employees? What can management do to address these potential employee problems?

STORY-SPECIFIC QUESTIONS

1. What are three lessons that a manager can learn from Purple Moon?
2. What were the possible benefits to society of the failed company?
3. Ventures like the Purple Moon may be, in part, responsible for a portion of the fact that the "girl"-related CD-ROM market expanded 38 percent last year. What are two things that Purple Moon should have done differently?

SHORT APPLICATION ASSIGNMENTS

1. In teams or individually, answer the story-specific questions; keep your answers to 25–75 words for each question.
2. In teams of three to five persons, or as a whole class, discuss your responses to the critical thinking questions.
3. Prepare a one-page memo report (200–250 words) to your instructor in which you summarize this article. You will find a model one-page report on the Web site (nytimes.swcollege.com).
4. Write an executive summary (200–250 words). As an administrative assistant to a busy executive, you are expected to summarize selected articles and present important points. You will find a model executive summary on the Web site.
5. Summarize this article (100–125 words) for your company's newsletter. You will find a model newsletter article on the Web site.
6. Write an essay (200–300 words) explicating the pros and cons of market research. Or, alternatively, prepare a class debate with one side advocating market research and the other side detailing the limitations of market research.

BUILDING RESEARCH SKILLS

1. Individually or in teams, research the Web site of Mattel Inc. and its competitors. What do they manufacture and market? Are they diversified? Who are their competitors? Who owns Mattel? How are these companies vertically integrated? Your instructor may ask you to submit a three- to five-page essay, post a Web page or report your results in a five-minute presentation, along with a letter of transmittal explaining your results.
2. If you were asked to develop a business plan for a new venture such as the Purple Moon, what specific problem areas would you address? Why? Your instructor also may ask you to submit a three- to five-page business plan or post a Web page explaining your business plan, along with a letter of transmittal explaining your results.
3. Individually or in teams, search for further evidence to support Purple Moon's assumption; namely, that games designed for boys may be perceived as "tedious" by young women. Your instructor may ask you to submit a three- to five-page essay, post a Web page or report your results in a five-minute presentation, along with a letter of transmittal explaining your results.
4. Using at least three other references (e.g., books, research-journal articles, newspaper or magazine stories or credible Web sites), post an 800- to 1,000-word Web

page that addresses two of the earlier critical thinking questions. Assume that your Web page will be used as an internal reference for a corporation's intranet.

5. Using at least three other references (e.g., books, research-journal articles, newspaper or magazine stories or credible Web sites), write an 800- to 1,000-word essay that addresses two of the earlier critical thinking questions. Assume that your essay will be used as an internal reference for a corporation's business plan.

CHAPTER 2

Managing Human Resources in a Changing Workplace

PREVIEW

Litigation, labor problems, diversity, rapid turnover and competition between "temps" and permanent employees are but a few of the problems that managers confront in today's rapidly changing workplace. A solution to these problems remains an unanswered question, "a work in progress."

The articles in this chapter illustrate the breadth, complexity and trends in today's work environment, as well as examine popular conceptions of the workplace. For example, Pam Belluck in "Maybe 'Rages' Aren't What They're Cracked Up to Be," questions the prevalence of workplace violence. Is it a real trend or one manufactured by news-media coverage? Next, Richard A. Oppel Jr., in his "Retaliation Lawsuits Are a Treacherous Slope," investigates the paradox of managers being sued for attempting to create a harassment and discrimination free workplace.

Steven Greenhouse's article "Why Labor Feels It Can't Afford to Lose This Strike" reviews the role of labor unions in a changing workplace. The International Brotherhood of Teamsters strike against United Parcel Service, better known as UPS, is the "first crusade against what many economists call the contingent economy, and what many business critics call corporate America's scaling back of its responsibilities to employees."

This chapter concludes with Abby Ellin's "I Want to Be a Chairborne Ranger: Boot Camp for the Office,"

The public sympathsizes with part-timers. Teamsters rally in New Jersey.

Source: Ozier Muhammed/The New York Times

which offers a snapshot of an innovative approach to coping with growing workplace complexity: employee survival training. Effective management today is akin to shooting "a moving target"—what worked a moment ago may now be "off-the-mark."

Maybe "Rages" Aren't What They're Cracked Up to Be

By Pam Belluck

When securities day trader Mark Barton walked into two Atlanta brokerage firms Thursday and fatally shot nine people, it seemed like another gruesome indicator of a trend toward workplace violence and rage.

Barton, 44, had traded with at least one of the firms and had apparently experienced significant financial losses in recent weeks, investigators said. In a note left behind after he took his own life, Barton said he wanted to kill "the people that greedily sought my destruction."

But it is not clear that what has been dubbed "workplace rage" is really on the rise, researchers say. And similar doubts have been raised about other so-called "rages," namely road rage and air rage. Some experts suggest that the labels reflect only a national penchant for lumping similar but isolated acts of violence into categories—and question whether media coverage is making them appear to be bona fide trends.

"Basically, what's going on is that anecdotes are being christened as trends," said Barry Glassner, a professor of sociology at the University of Southern California and the author of *The Culture of Fear: Why Americans Are Afraid of the Wrong Things*, published in June by Basic Books. "There is no reason to believe that we have any new alarming situation in American society."

Glassner said such problems get wide publicity in part because of television news, which thrives on showing chilling footage of each new act of public rage, and because politicians and others use them to advance their own agendas. "There are lots of people making money off of these scares," he said.

Some psychologists say these are not spurious trends, but the natural consequences of more drivers on the road and more passengers in the air. Some, like Dr. Ervin Staub, a professor of psychology at the University of Massachusetts, attribute them to the decline of close communities and accelerating changes in society that make people more frustrated and angry.

Still others say that regardless of how many incidents there actually are, the labels serve the useful purpose of raising awareness about a problem and making people more careful about their safety. After all, drunken driving was common long before Mothers Against Drunk Driving came into existence, but it wasn't until after the group's formation that society began to seriously focus on the problem and take significant steps to curb it.

Yet a lot of skeptics tend to agree with Dr. Robert Baron, a professor of management and psychology at the Rensselaer Polytechnic Institute, who says, "All these social phenomena, they're just as slippery as eels."

Baron, whose expertise is workplace violence, said: "A lot of people are convinced there's a heck of a lot more than there used to be. But there isn't, from all the statistics that are out there."

Gallup polls conducted for the last four years on workplace anger show no increase in percentages of people who report feeling angry at work, said Batia Wiesenfeld, an assistant professor of management at New York University, who helped conduct the polls. Only 2 percent reported feeling extremely angry, while under 10 percent reported feeling "quite a bit angry," she said.

"The rates of anger are not extraordinarily high and they have not been changing that much over the past few years," Wiesenfeld said.

With air rage and road rage, there may be similar gaps between perception and reality. Two weeks ago, after an airline passenger severely beat a Continental Airlines gate agent at Newark International Airport, airline workers organized protests to demand that airlines do more to protect their employees from what they said were increasing incidents of passengers punching, kicking and biting.

There have certainly been some high-profile cases of alarming passenger behavior in recent years—most notoriously the 1995 incident in which a banker from Greenwich, Connecticut, assaulted a flight attendant and defecated on a food cart on a flight from Buenos Aires to New York.

But while airlines report a growing problem, it may be attributable to significant increases in the number of airline passengers rather than a higher rate of unruly passenger behavior. And definitions of unruly behavior vary from airline to airline, and can run the gamut from verbal abuse to assault. While their statistics are not exhaustive, federal aviation authorities have recorded only about 200 incidents in which passengers interfered with flight crews, about one for every 3 million passengers.

With road rage, the numbers seem to vary considerably, depending on the definition of terms like "aggressive driver."

Dr. Arnold Nerenberg, the clinical psychologist who popularized the term road rage, has a Web site, www.roadrage.com, that makes some alarming statements, like, "Twenty-eight thousand Americans died in 1996 because of aggressive driving," and, "There are estimated to be close to two billion episodes of road rage per year in our nation."

The 28,000 figure comes from 1997 congressional testimony by the head of the National Highway Traffic Safety Administration, who said that aggressive behavior included tailgating, passing on the right, flashing headlights to pass a car, weaving through busy lanes, honking or screaming at other drivers and exchanges of insults. The testimony indicated that such behavior was a factor in nearly 28,000 deaths—not the sole cause.

At that same hearing, Nerenberg testified that a survey he conducted of 585 drivers had found that 53 percent of drivers had "road rage disorder," which he described as one driver's clearly expressing anger to another at least twice a year.

Glassner said one consequence of inventing a term like road rage is that it is self-perpetuating; more incidents are reported because people suddenly have a category to group them in.

Another consequence is that people become more concerned about their own safety.

Dr. Ronald Nathan, a psychologist at Albany Medical College, sells an audio tape called "Road Rage Readiness," that dispenses pointers like who is most likely to engage in it (young men in high-performance cars, he says). He also offers exercises designed to help drivers control their frustration over, say, being cut off by an aggressive driver.

His training approach has altered over time to reflect what he suggests is increasing fear about road rage.

"At first I used to teach people to think that there might be some really good reason for the person to cut us off—maybe he had to get to the hospital," Nathan said. But now he teaches people "to assume the worst—that the road-rager has a gun on seat next to them and would use it."

The most distressing consequence of the "rage" trends, critics say, is that they take attention away from dangers that are clearly much more common: drunken driving fatalities, for example, or injuries suffered on the job.

"Those things are a lot more preventable too," Glassner said. "How do you imagine that you're going to prevent somebody who is going off the deep end from getting violent in the workplace? What disturbs me about this attention to these pseudophenomena is that we lose focus on what is really out there."

The New York Times, August 1, 1999
http://www.nytimes.com/library/review/080199rage-review.html

CRITICAL THINKING QUESTIONS

1. With the unprecedented wealth and security afforded to the average American, why would someone engage in an act of workplace violence?
2. Is road, air or workplace rage ever justified? Why, or why not?
3. Why will road, air or workplace rage decrease or increase in the future?

STORY-SPECIFIC QUESTIONS

1. Give two reasons why some experts suggest that the phenomenon of workplace rage, like other forms of rage, is really on the rise.
2. Glassner suggests that the "rage" phenomenon may also be related to what factor?
3. What does the Gallup poll report about "rage" as a growing trend?
4. According to Glassner, what is one consequence of inventing a term like "road rage?"
5. According to the article, what useful purposes might these "rage" labels serve?

SHORT APPLICATION ASSIGNMENTS

1. In teams or individually, answer the story-specific questions; keep your answers to 25–75 words for each question.
2. In teams of three to five persons, or as a whole class, discuss your responses to the critical thinking questions.
3. Prepare a one-page memo report (200–250 words) to your instructor in which you summarize this article. You will find a model one-page report on the Web site (nytimes.swcollege.com).
4. Write an executive summary (200–250 words). As an administrative assistant to a busy executive, you are expected to summarize selected articles and present important points. You will find a model executive summary on the Web site.
5. Summarize this article (100–125 words) for your company's newsletter. You will find a model newsletter article on the Web site.

BUILDING RESEARCH SKILLS

1. Research three cases of workplace rage. Why do you agree or disagree with the author's thesis that rage may not be the trend that it has been made out to be? Your instructor may ask you to submit a three- to five-page essay, post a Web page or report your results in a five-minute presentation, along with a letter of transmittal explaining your findings.
2. Using at least three other references (e.g., books, research-journal articles, newspaper or magazine stories or credible Web sites), write an 800- to 1,000-word essay that addresses two of the earlier critical thinking questions. Assume that your essay will be used as an internal reference for a corporation's marketing plan.
3. Using at least three other references (e.g., books, research-journal articles, newspaper or magazine stories or credible Web sites), post an 800- to 1,000-word Web page that addresses at least two of the earlier critical thinking questions. Assume that your page will be posted in the marketing section of a corporate intranet.

Retaliation Lawsuits Are a Treacherous Slope

By Richard A. Oppel Jr.

Corporate managers handle sexual harassment complaints all the time. Think the following example is a no-brainer? Think again.

After a woman who worked as a receptionist at the Birmingham, Alabama, office of the Dillard Paper Company sued the company, another employee there, Harry Merritt, acknowledged in a deposition that he had told her that since a certain customer "sure is taken with you, why don't you take care of him sometime?" according to a court opinion. He also acknowledged having repeatedly used a vulgar phrase telling her to scratch a part of his anatomy.

Merritt contended that he had not harassed the woman. Shortly after the company settled the receptionist's lawsuit, though, he was dismissed. He said his boss told him, "Your deposition was the most damning to Dillard's case, and you no longer have a place here."

Merritt sued, arguing that he had been wrongfully terminated in retaliation for his testimony, which the company had told him to provide. A Federal district court threw out the case. But an appeals court reinstated it, and Dillard settled the dispute last year, during the trial, for an undisclosed sum.

How could a company find itself in legal trouble for dismissing an employee for behavior admitted to in sworn testimony?

Easily, it turns out. For although many employers have become more sophisticated about responding to explicit charges of sexual, racial or age discrimination, they often get tripped up in the legal labyrinth that ensues. The most common mistake is to dismiss or discipline an employee for what the company regards as real misdeeds, only to be accused of punishing him or her for filing a discrimination claim or lawsuit. And many have discovered to their consternation that juries will award damages for such supposed retaliation, even if they believe the discrimination charges are bogus.

But that is not the only trap. As Merritt's case makes clear, lawsuits can draw in other employees, who must testify under oath to lawyers from both sides. As Dillard Paper learned to its regret, under Federal civil rights law, such employees' statements cannot be held against them, no matter what they say.

Retaliation suits are "like an iceberg, a hidden claim that a lot of people don't know how to handle," said Michael P. Maslanka, a partner at Clark, West, Keller, Butler & Ellis in Dallas. "Retaliation resonates with the jury. They may not believe the employer terminated someone because they are black, but they will believe they terminated someone because they rocked the boat."

The paradox of using a law that was enacted to protect victims of discrimination to benefit plaintiffs who make groundless charges or employees who admit to offensive behavior was not lost on judges for the United States Court of Appeals for the 11th Circuit, in Atlanta, who upheld Merritt's right to a trial.

"We recognize that our holding allows a man who admitted to engaging in sexual harassment to take his termination case to a jury," Judge Edward E. Carnes wrote. "We are emphatically not holding, however, that an alleged sexual harasser cannot be fired"—only that the dismissal cannot be based on the harasser's participation in a civil rights law proceeding, his opinion stated.

In an interview last week, Merritt said he was dismissed "for telling the truth." He also contended that the receptionist had "made a lot of allegations about me that were untrue" and that "lots of things were taken out of context." Officials at Dillard Paper, which is now part of Xpedx, a unit of the International Paper Company, confirmed that a settlement had been reached.

The number of civil rights employment lawsuits filed in Federal courts has stabilized in recent years at around 23,000 annually after sharply rising in the mid-1990s, partly because the tight labor market has made bosses more eager to keep their workers happy.

But lawsuits by employees contending that their bosses retaliated against them for filing or aiding discrimination claims still prove nettlesome for many managers. Retaliation claims now account for 24 percent of all charges filed with the Equal Employment Opportunity Commission, up from 15 percent in 1992. Employment law experts say juries are far more likely to believe charges of retaliation—thus making decisions to dismiss or discipline employees who have already filed discrimination charges legally treacherous, no matter what the facts are.

Many managers "may not realize that retaliation does not require a valid underlying claim," said John D. Canoni, a partner at the Nixon Peabody law firm in New York. "You can have a complaint that's totally bogus, unfounded and unrealistic, but if someone reacts against you because of that claim, even if it was bogus," you can win a retaliation suit, he said.

In fact, over the last five years, employers lost a higher percentage of retaliation lawsuits than of cases that accused them of discrimination because of age, disability, race or sex, according to Jury Verdict Research, a legal research firm and publisher in Horsham, Pennsylvania.

So what are the lessons for employers? In a nutshell: get rid of problem employees quickly. Be aware that some employees might file discrimination claims or lawsuits in an effort to protect their jobs. If they do, and if you dismiss or discipline them later, be sure to base your decision on facts collected independently by you and be sure *not* to cite depositions or anything else connected with their lawsuits.

As an example of how badly things can go awry if employers are careless, legal experts point to a ruling this year in which the Court of Appeals for the 10th Circuit, in Denver, upheld a jury award of $460,132 to an employee of

Ortho Biotech Inc. who a jury found was dismissed in retaliation for filing race discrimination charges against the company.

According to the appeals court opinion, the employee, Oliver Medlock Jr., had a number of contentious encounters with his bosses before he filed the equal-employment charges and, later, a discrimination lawsuit. At one point, Medlock confronted a supervisor after a meeting, accused him of building a file of inaccurate information and threatened him physically if he continued. Other conflicts ensued, but Ortho's senior managers did not act on a recommendation from Medlock's boss that he be dismissed.

After Medlock filed his lawsuit, he was interviewed by the company's lawyers in a deposition. A month later, he was suspended, and soon after that he was dismissed. As Ortho explained in a letter: "As a result of issues raised in your deposition, effective immediately, you are suspended from all duties on behalf of the company."

Big mistake. The letter provided Medlock ammunition that his actual dismissal was in response to his discrimination charge. Indeed, a jury found against Medlock on every claim but one—retaliation.

The appeals court upheld the award in January. "Taken in the light most favorable to plaintiff, we must conclude the letters, coupled with the close temporal proximity between plaintiff's deposition and firing, directly support the jury's finding that defendant terminated plaintiff in retaliation" for his discrimination claim, wrote Judge Carlos Lucero. The company has appealed to the Supreme Court.

The New York Times, September 29, 1999

http://www.nytimes.com/library/financial/092999manage-harass.html

CRITICAL THINKING QUESTIONS

1. Some argue that the law has gone "too far" in its efforts to protect employees. What arguments could you develop to support this position?
2. Some argue that the law has "not gone far enough" in its efforts to protect employees. What arguments could you develop to support this position?
3. The story illustrates how "common sense" is not always the best approach to managing people. Name other examples in which effective management and "common sense" may not go hand-in-hand.

STORY-SPECIFIC QUESTIONS

1. The author suggests that the rise in civil rights employment lawsuits filed in Federal courts has stabilized because of what factor?
2. What is the most common mistake a company can make to land itself in legal trouble for dismissing an employee for behavior admitted to in sworn testimony?

3. What paradox do retaliation lawsuits pose for managers?
4. What did Judge Carnes write concerning the Merritt case?

SHORT APPLICATION ASSIGNMENTS

1. In teams or individually, answer the story-specific questions; keep your answers to 25–75 words for each question.
2. In teams of three to five persons, or as a whole class, discuss your responses to the critical thinking questions.
3. Prepare a one-page memo report (200–250 words) to your instructor in which you summarize this article. You will find a model one-page report on the Web site (nytimes.swcollege.com).
4. Write an executive summary (200–250 words). As an administrative assistant to a busy executive, you are expected to summarize selected articles and present important points. You will find a model executive summary on the Web site.
5. Summarize this article (100–125 words) for your company's newsletter. You will find a model newsletter article on the Web site.
6. In teams of three to five persons, or as a whole class, develop a company policy for sexual harassment. Be prepared to present and defend your policy with the class.

BUILDING RESEARCH SKILLS

1. Individually or in teams, investigate how your institution informs its employees of its harassment and discrimination policies. Are the training and procedures used adequate in the eyes of managers? Interview several managers regarding their knowledge of harassment and discrimination policies, and of the steps they need to take to protect themselves and their employees. Make certain that their responses are kept anonymous. Your instructor may ask you to submit a three- to five-page essay, post a Web page or report your results in a five-minute presentation, along with a letter of transmittal explaining how the project.
2. Individually or in teams, draft a step-by-process for handling difficult employees. Your instructor may give you a sample company. Your instructor also may ask you to submit a three- to five-page policy manual or post a Web page, along with a letter of transmittal explaining the project.
3. Individually or in teams, analyze the sexual harassment, age or racial discrimination policies at your institution. Or your instructor may give you a sample institution. You also may be asked to submit a three- to five-page paper or post a Web page summarizing your findings.
4. Using at least three other references (e.g., books, research-journal articles, newspaper or magazine stories or credible Web sites), write an 800- to 1,000-word essay that addresses two of the earlier critical thinking questions. Assume that your essay will be used as an internal reference for a corporation's marketing plan.
5. Using at least three other references (e.g., books, research-journal articles, newspaper or magazine stories or credible Web sites), post an 800- to 1,000-word Web page that addresses at least two of the earlier critical thinking questions. Assume that your page will be posted in the marketing section of a corporate intranet.

Why Labor Feels It Can't Afford to Lose This Strike

By Steven Greenhouse

For years American workers have grumbled about downsizing, the rise in part-time and temporary jobs, and the trend toward businesses offering fewer workers health insurance and pensions. But they did little to protest that cost-cutting—until now.

The mighty International Brotherhood of Teamsters, in its strike against the United Parcel Service, has mounted the first crusade against what many economists call "the contingent economy," and what many business critics call corporate America's scaling back of its responsibilities to employees.

But while the teamsters' labor allies praise the union for fighting for more full-time jobs with full benefits at UPS, some labor experts say that if the teamsters win big, victory could be a mixed blessing.

On the one hand, a union victory would be an important signal that AFL-CIO president John J. Sweeney has re-energized the labor movement, encouraging some of the 85 percent of the workforce that isn't unionized to think more about joining.

On the other hand, even with a teamster victory, the strike could ultimately hurt job opportunities and job security at UPS, the world's largest package deliverer, and one with a good record in dealing with organized labor.

If the teamsters achieve a big victory in terms of higher wages and greater restrictions on UPS' use of part-timers, that could push up the shipper's costs, pushing business even after the strike to competitors that are largely non-union (the major exception is the Postal Service) and that also rely on lots of part-time workers.

UPS executives have repeatedly boasted that the company has been a job-creating machine over the last four years, adding 46,000 unionized jobs. But the teamsters complain that 38,000 of those new jobs were part-time, paying too little to support a family.

Last week, UPS chairman James Kelly warned that the company would have to lay off 15,000 of its 185,000 teamster employees because of business lost from the strike. While teamster officials angrily called that warning an exaggeration and "intimidation," economists say that lost market share, and the accompanying loss of some jobs, is a result of many strikes.

"Every customer whose life has been turned upside down by the UPS strike might think about using a shipper where there won't be strikes," said Paul Schlesinger, a transportation analyst at Donaldson, Lufkin & Jenrette. "If the strike slows the growth of the UPS job machine, it's going to hurt the teamsters."

In addition, the increased wages and the restrictions on part-time jobs sought by the union could make UPS less competitive against Federal Express, DHL Worldwide and other competitors, particularly in the overnight shipping business that UPS has fought so hard to enter, and which is so dependent on part-timers.

Ever since UPS' teamster members walked out August 4, company officials have said that the union's demands would make the company uncompetitive and cost it customers. That suggested an analogy to the high wages of auto workers helping Japanese car manufacturers make huge inroads in the 1970s and 1980s, causing the loss of many auto workers' jobs.

In their defense, teamster officials say their wage demands are modest and should not cause UPS to become uncompetitive, especially since the company's relatively high profit margins give it room to lower prices. In addition, teamster officials contend that their demands to restrict the number of part-time jobs shouldn't make the company less competitive than a prime rival like Federal Express, because while two-fifths of Federal Express workers are part-time, three-fifths of UPS workers are.

Sweeney of the AFL-CIO said the teamsters' focus on improving working conditions for part-timers might pressure other employers, unionized or non-unionized, to treat them better. Not surprisingly, he also said that the teamsters' fight, especially if victorious, would make more part-time workers interested in joining unions—and more unions interested in organizing them.

"This has raised the level of focus on part-time workers and that's why companies that use a lot of part-timers, like Sears Roebuck, have been urging UPS to hang tough," he said.

But some labor experts say Sweeney is overly optimistic if he thinks legions of part-timers will join unions in response to the strike. According to the Bureau of Labor Statistics, 23.2 million Americans—18.3 percent of the workforce—work part time.

"Certainly a teamster victory would encourage part-time workers to be a little more interested in unions," said Richard Hurd, a professor of labor relations at Cornell University. "But part-time workers have a high turnover and have been very hard to organize historically. Even though the strike could improve labor's image, I wouldn't imagine many major incursions into the part-time market."

Another hope of labor is that a victory would encourage workers at Federal Express and other shippers to think that a union could help them. A big obstacle to organizing Federal Express, however, is its successful lobbying last year to be placed under the Railway Labor Act, instead of the National Labor Relations Act.

Under the railway act, which generally covers airlines and railroads, a union can organize workers only by having representation elections for all of a company's workers at once, instead of conducting separate elections at individual sites. It would be a tall order to organize Federal Express' 110,000 workers all at once.

"I'm not sure precisely how a victory at UPS would enable the teamsters to conquer Federal Express or UPS' other non-union competitors," said Melvyn Dubofsky, a labor historian at the State University of New York at Binghamton.

"Symbolically, a teamsters' victory would be very very important because so many of the other major labor battles of the past five or six years, like Caterpillar, were largely defeats."

The New York Times, August 17, 1997
http://www.nytimes.com/library/review/081797labor-review.html

CRITICAL THINKING QUESTIONS

1. In your opinion, how have labor unions benefited workers?
2. In your opinion, how have labor unions hurt the interests of workers?
3. Are part-time workers a viable union target? Why, or why not? Are the unions wasting time trying to recruit part-time workers?
4. How, if at all, will unions evolve in relation to such workplace issues as technology, diversification and globalization?

STORY-SPECIFIC QUESTIONS

1. According to the story, what percent of the American workforce is non-union?
2. List three benefits for labor unions from a possible teamster victory over UPS.
3. What are two potential problems for UPS and its workers if the teamsters achieve a big victory in terms of higher wages and greater restrictions on the use of part-time workers by UPS?

SHORT APPLICATION ASSIGNMENTS

1. In teams or individually, answer the story-specific questions; keep your answers to 25–75 words for each question.
2. In teams of three to five persons, or as a whole class, discuss your responses to the critical thinking questions.
3. Prepare a one-page memo report (200–250 words) to your instructor in which you summarize this article. You will find a model one-page report on the Web site (nytimes.swcollege.com).
4. Write an executive summary (200–250 words). As an administrative assistant to a busy executive, you are expected to summarize selected articles and present important points. You will find a model executive summary on the Web site.
5. Summarize this article (100–125 words) for your company's newsletter. You will find a model newsletter article on the Web site.
6. Individually or in teams, investigate a labor union in your area. What are the costs

and benefits of joining? Is the union's membership growing or shrinking? Your instructor may ask you to present your findings in an oral report or submit a 150- to 200-word summary.

BUILDING RESEARCH SKILLS

1. Since this story was written, UPS and the teamsters settled the strike. What was the outcome? How has it impacted the company? Your instructor may ask you to present your findings in an oral report or submit a three- to five-page summary.
2. Temporary workers in other areas of the economy, especially technology, have considered unionizing. Individually or in teams, investigate the success or failure of a company or industry. Your instructor may give you a sample company or industry. Your instructor may ask you to submit a three- to five-page essay, post a Web page or report your results in a five-minute presentation, along with a letter of transmittal explaining your findings.
3. Using at least three other references (e.g., books, research-journal articles, newspaper or magazine stories or credible Web sites), write an 800- to 1,000-word essay that addresses two of the earlier critical thinking questions. Assume that your essay will be used as an internal reference for a corporation's human resources department.
4. Using at least three other references (e.g., books, research-journal articles, newspaper or magazine stories or credible Web sites), post an 800- to 1,000-word Web page that addresses at least two of the earlier critical thinking questions. Assume that your page will be posted in the human resources section of a corporate intranet.

I Want to Be a Chairborne Ranger: Boot Camp for the Office

By Abby Ellin

Mannsville, Kentucky—It's Thursday afternoon, the rain is rattling rooftops and workers from the Vandor Corp. are huddled in a tent in the middle of nowhere, dressed in Army fatigues and combat boots.

One of them is about to be named platoon leader, the person in charge, and right now they all wish they were invisible.

The man responsible for their unease, a former Army Ranger named Dean Hohl, raises an index finger and looks toward Jeanne Steffen, 30, the receptionist at Vandor, a diversified manufacturer in Richmond, Ind.

Her face is a mask of horror. "Why me?" she says. "I don't want to do it."

Hohl smiles. That's precisely the point.

He issues helmets, canteens and paintball guns, warning the workers—among them the general manager, a mold maker, a document controller and a maintenance man—to keep them pointed down. "Remember," he cautions, "friendly fire isn't."

Hohl, who is 28, leads the 11 workers into the woods to familiarize them with the terrain, which is slick, muddy and largely uphill. People huff. They sweat. They wipe the condensation from their helmets. They return to the tent soggy and waterlogged, boots drenched.

Ms. Steffen is confused. "I guess there's a reason for this," she says. "There'd better be."

It's Day One for the Vandor workers in a four-day, three-night team-building program run by Hohl and his best friend, Shane Dozier, also 28 and an ex-Ranger. (Rangers are the guys who jumped out of planes in Panama and carried out rescue missions in Grenada.)

Programs like this one—along with Outward Bound, ropes classes and others with more than a hint of summer-camp color wars—have become almost ubiquitous in the world of corporate training.

But Hohl and Dozier go beyond the norm. Their 96-hour training session does not end until tears have been shed, confidence has been shattered and bodies and egos have been bruised—all for the sake of building the corporate team.

"Basically, we've created a vehicle that transfers the time-tested principles of the military into everyday business," said Hohl, whose company, Leading Concepts is based in Louisville and operates the camp here, about 65 miles southeast.

"In my world as a Ranger, if you screw up, you die."

Why go to such extremes to train office workers? Do paintball wars and military meals build more effective work units than a well-designed trust walk?

"You don't go back into the workplace and fall into each others' arms," Hohl said. Like work itself, "this is much more intensive. It's a real in-your-face experience."

So far, he has trained nearly 500 people at corporations like Blue Cross and Blue Shield of Illinois, DJ/Nypro, a plastics company in Louisville, and Vandor.

Last week, Domino's Pizza sent its first group into the woods.

4 P.M. THURSDAY

Back at "headquarters"—a tent with rows of benches, overhead lanterns, a makeshift stove and the trainer's indispensable weapon, a flip chart—the group shivers and smokes.

Dozier, a mass of white teeth and piercing blue eyes whose face is smeared with greasepaint, has the Vandor workers explain why they have volunteered to drive four and a half hours from home and work to live in the mud.

"I'm here to move up in the company," one woman says. "To challenge myself," someone else says. "To learn how to communicate better and be a team," another says.

The latter, of course, is Vandor's reason for spending about $2,300 a head on the training. Five years ago, the company divided its 110 employees into teams. It held seminars and brought in leadership experts, but employees didn't quite get it.

("What we missed, badly, was that everyone has a different experience: Some have never been on a team, some have been on championship teams, some have been on teams that failed or lost," said John D. Wayne, executive vice president, who took the Leading Concepts course last year. "We didn't address questions like what changes on a day-to-day basis now that we're a team. We knew that companies who adopt the team philosophy do better, and we were looking for a way to make it work when we came across this.")

Hohl explains the drill. Each day, the group will go on a series of 1½-hour missions. The enemy is known as Modd, for "make our day difficult," real-live humans who, like the workers, are armed with real-live paintballs. One mission might be to raid Modd headquarters and steal their weapons; another might be to hover by their camp and observe.

Modd is a metaphor for workday stresses. "Every day at work you're on a mission with a team, a goal and a Modd," Hohl says. "Your job is to figure out how to deal with it. Make sense?"

The group nods, but the fact is, they are hopelessly lost—as any worker might be on the first day on a new job. They break for a 10-minute latrine run. The rain has turned to hail.

9 P.M. THURSDAY

Before leaving for the night, Hohl hands out the dinner—MRE, or meals ready to eat: chili macaroni or beef stew, a packet of applesauce, pound cake, crackers, jelly and a sugary powder that the Vandor employees pour into their mouths like Pixy Stix. Dozier sets out two kerosene heaters; people take turns drying their pants, shirts and socks.

While they eat, Ms. Steffen tries to relay the next morning's mission—to claim their new supplies from Modd camp without getting shot. Her colleagues are chattering, swapping cigarettes and gum, and she loses her cool. "You're not listening!" she cries. "We're supposed to be a team.'

"Well, I'm not perfect," one man says.

"I just don't understand anything that's happening," another says.

"God, I don't want this responsibility!' says Ms. Steffen, looking down at her paperwork. "But if you don't help me we're going to be here all night."

They decide to split into groups to plan the mission, breaking it down into its components. It takes about an hour, but they build a strategy. Slowly, they are learning the meaning of "team."

6 A.M. FRIDAY

Tired, cranky, damp and cold, the workers buckle their helmets, test-fire their guns and head into the woods. Dodging snipers, firing rounds and ducking behind trees is surprisingly addictive; the shouts of joy when someone smacks a Modd with a paintball are infectious.

During the debriefing, Ms. Steffen says she feels a little better than yesterday, but still inadequate, inexperienced and ill-suited to leadership.

1:45 P.M. FRIDAY

Hohl lectures about the emotional cycle of change and people's resistance to it. He summarizes research that concluded success was based not on I.Q. or education, but on the ability to establish rapport with others. The speech seems a little obvious—Werner Erhard goes to the woods—and Hohl acknowledges that none of this is brain surgery.

Dozier lays out the next mission: to gather information on the Modd members—what they're wearing, how many there are, what kind of equipment they have. People eagerly sit down to figure out tactics and strategies.

7:15 P.M. FRIDAY

The group is pumped, ready to shoot the Modd to pieces. "Let's kick their butts!" Ms. Steffen shouts.

And then the unthinkable happens. As they prepare to leave camp, Dozier switches assignments. The new platoon leader is Bill Byrd, 23, a maintenance technician who is flabbergasted at the news. His immediate boss is here, which means he will be his boss' boss. This is no longer fun.

The squad members return an hour and a half later, splattered with paint and mud, looking as if they have been to hell and back. The Modd beat them mercilessly, ambushing them with bigger and better equipment.

Those in the front of the line, close to Byrd, felt confident, but those in the back did not get the right information to know what they were doing.

"Ever get that at work?" Hohl asks. "When you're close to the top, you know what's up. But often, the rest of the group doesn't. That's why it's so important to communicate."

Byrd looks as if he is about to cry. "We failed because of my ignorance, and I seriously apologize to Jeanne for anything I might have said about her," he says. "I realize how hard your first day was."

"None of us could have done any better," says John Spadavecchia, 39, Vandor's general manager.

People are pensive, trying to connect this experience to work.

"You did this to prove a point," says Nancy Hines, 49, a Vandor team leader, or supervisor. "Don't get too comfortable. Things change."

Vella Johnson, also 49, a customer service representative, adds: "If you're not clear on what you're doing, you're going to make a mess of everything."

As for Ms. Steffen, a funny thing has happened; she has realized that people needed her help.

"I kept trying to say, 'we're not ready,' but everyone wanted to go," she says. "After being in the leadership role and having to step back, it was frustrating, because I was the only one who knew what to do, and I wanted to do it."

Hohl steps in. "You've got to be prepared," he says. "You can't be afraid to ask for help—or offer it. And you always need to know what other people are doing in their jobs."

7 A.M. SATURDAY

Patches of sunlight are finally peeking through the clouds, and morale is a little higher. The previous night, Byrd had sought Ms. Steffen's help; now, raring to go, he discusses the plan again.

But right before they head out, Dozier pulls another fast one. The new platoon leader is Spadavecchia, and Byrd is crushed.

Still, the group performs flawlessly—few casualties, and many direct hits on the Modd. Words like "teamwork," "planning," and "communication" pop up during the post-mortem.

Dozier beams. "As a team, you can overcome any obstacle if you plan for it," he says. "Y'all learned the hard way."

Later, Hohl talks about conflict and its role in relationships. He scribbles four words on his flip chart: Forming. Storming. Norming. Performing.

"Storming's the bickering and arguing among team members," he says. "When this happens, people often say, 'OK, we don't get along—guess we'd better change teams.' But real teams aren't about 'Do we like each other?' They're about 'Can we respect the diversity—do we have the skill sets covered at all the bases within the team?' Anything can knock you down—a new member comes in, you get a leader who communicates differently. What the team's got to be good at is getting through it."

5:30 P.M. SATURDAY

Dozier is reviewing the afternoon's mission: attack the Modd camp and steal supplies. Everyone tries to listen, but they are tired and hungry, busy examining their bruises; paintballs hurt. And after the morning's success, maybe they are a little cocksure.

An hour later they head into the woods single file, whispering, dropping to the ground, firing at the Modd. Then, right in the middle of it, Dozier switches leaders again. Now the man in charge is David Collins, 44, a computer moldmaker.

The change knocks everyone off balance. Collins yells orders. The team implodes.

Back at camp, no one looks at anyone else. Clearly, they are battling the worst kind of Modd—an internal one, having to do with power struggles, lack of trust, blame.

"Y'all are having problems communicating," Dozier says. "I suggest you figure it out, or you're not going to make it."

They beg him to stick around, to moderate, but he refuses. "I have faith," he says, turning away. "Talk it through."

Everyone is a little stunned until Spadavecchia volunteers to facilitate. He has proved himself trustworthy and thoughtful, a solid communicator; that could be why he is the general manager.

One by one, people say how they felt during the mission: Angry. Confused. Lost. Alone. They point accusing fingers at Collins and tell him not to talk down to them. He apologizes, saying he might have been overzealous in playing his role.

It is very intense, very painful. Nearly fours hours later, people are wiping their eyes and looking as if they have been through combat. But people have spoken. And asked questions. And listened.

NOON SUNDAY

The final mission is to "search and destroy" the Modd, and the team embraces it with glee. Given the choice, they appoint Spadavecchia as platoon leader.

Everyone works in sync—shooting the Modd, stealing guns, rescuing fallen team members.

At the end of the day, the Modd—which turns out to be five men, mostly friends of Dozier and Hohl—emerge from the woods. They pull off their helmets, and everyone lets out a whoop. There, before them, is their boss, Wayne. The workers are all visibly moved that Wayne was around to witness their success. They had met the Modd—personal demons, external foes, even, in a way, their employer—and conquered it.

EPILOGUE

Back at Vandor, the group retains its high. A week after the out-of-office experience, workers are still checking in with one another regularly, communicating when conflicts arise. It is not uncommon, Hohl says, for people to go home re-evaluating all their relationships, not just those at work.

Vandor is trying to transform the office into one big platoon. Lists of Leading Concepts terminology hang on the walls, and there is a formal network of program graduates. Hohl and Dozier also do a year of follow-ups, offering supplemental audiotapes and motivational speeches.

Wayne says the training works miracles. "When you have good teamwork, it's pretty obvious, and when you don't, it's even more obvious," he says. "You get wiped out, shot. Now when you're back at work and something goes wrong, you can tie it back to the experience. You can say: 'It's about bad communication. It's like when we were on a raid, and I didn't understand the chain of command.'"

Still, leadership is not for everyone. Ms. Steffen, back at her reception desk, sums up her feelings: "It was a positive experience, and I'm glad I went through it with these people. But I wouldn't want to do it again."

The New York Times, May 24, 1998
http://www.nytimes.com/library/financial/sunday/052498earn-teamwork-camp.html

CRITICAL THINKING QUESTIONS

1. Why would management experiment with the training and indoctrination described in this story?
2. What could be the possible advantages and disadvantages of this training?
3. Is this boot camp training a passing fad? Why, or why not?
4. How would one justify the time and expense of this type of an outdoor training program?

STORY-SPECIFIC QUESTIONS

1. Compared to other outdoor team-building programs, what puts Holz and Dozier's model beyond the norm?
2. List three companies that have used this approach.
3. Briefly explain Storming.

SHORT APPLICATION ASSIGNMENTS

1. In teams or individually, answer the story-specific questions; keep your answers to 25–75 words for each question.
2. In teams of three to five persons, or as a whole class, discuss your responses to the critical thinking questions.
3. Prepare a one-page memo report (200–250 words) to your instructor in which you summarize this article. You will find a model one-page report on the Web site (nytimes.swcollege.com).
4. Write an executive summary (200–250 words). As an administrative assistant to a busy executive, you are expected to summarize selected articles and present important points. You will find a model executive summary on the Web site.
5. Summarize this article (100–125 words) for your company's newsletter. You will find a model newsletter article on the Web site.

BUILDING RESEARCH SKILLS

1. Ellin suggests that tamer yet similar experiences such as Outward Bound are "ubiquitous" in organizational settings. Use the World Wide Web to research what Outward Bound has to offer and compare this to the Boot Camp described in the story. Your instructor may ask you to present your findings in an oral report, submit a three- to five-page policy manual or post a Web page, along with a letter of transmittal explaining your results.
2. Using at least three other references (e.g., books, research-journal articles, newspaper or magazine stories or credible Web sites), write an 800- to 1,000-word essay that addresses two of the earlier critical thinking questions. Assume that your essay will be used as an internal reference for a corporation's human resource department.
3. Using at least three other references (e.g., books, research-journal articles, newspaper or magazine stories or credible Web sites), post an 800- to 1,000-word Web page that addresses at least two of the earlier critical thinking questions. Assume that your page will be posted in the human resource section of a corporate intranet.

The Role of Management Theory

PREVIEW

$\mathbf{M}$anagement theories come and go. Theories once regarded as "cutting edge" are now passé. Ironically, however, many of these dismissed theories are later resurrected. Although the following articles do not answer the question of why theories come and go, they do illustrate a crucial point: theories are borne out of necessity and remain in vogue until a new problem or solution emerges.

As Fred Andrews reports in "Peter Drucker Still Preaches Customers Over Profits," the purpose of business is to create customers. A pioneer in management theory, Drucker has done much to revolutionize and define what it means to be a manager. Nevertheless, he has fallen out of favor, with some now considering his ideas to be antiquated.

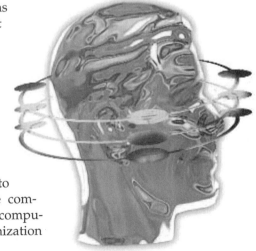

Chaos and complexity are two management theories now in fashion. When rational approaches fail, as Malcolm W. Browne explains in "Science Squints at a Future Fogged by Chaotic Uncertainty," it may be that some phenomenon cannot be predicted.

Or the opposite may be true, counters Steve Ditlea in "Applying Complexity Theory to Business Management." Managers could use complexity theory, the study of mathematical and computational principles of orderliness and self-organization in nature, to guide their decision-making.

Source: Christine M. Thompson/CyberTimes

Peter Drucker Still Preaches Customers Over Profits

By Fred Andrews

Corporate America and Dr. Peter Ferdinand Drucker have fallen out of favor with each other. Drucker still has his disciples, but at the bleeding edge of business the old master's lifework is commonly seen as simplistic, portentous, off the mark, idealistic, out of date. Not for 20 years have the corporate world's heavy hitters hung on his every word.

For his part, The Man Who Invented Corporate Society (a biographer's apt label) disdains a corporate order that is in thrall to stock prices and that rewards its chief executives as though they were power forwards. "Earnings per share" does not exist in Peter Drucker's vocabulary. The religion of shareholder supremacy has him shaking his head.

"That's right, I am not very happy with the unbalanced emphasis on stock price and market cap and short-term earnings," Drucker said in an interview last week. "The most critical management job is to balance short term and long term. In the long term, today's one-sided emphasis is deleterious and dangerous." (The saving grace, he added, is that many companies pay lip service to short-term shareholder interests. "Actually, they are much better managed," he said.)

To his thinking, two personages, the customer and the highly skilled employee, are at least as precious as the investor. Increasingly, as pension beneficiaries, owners of stock options or mutual fund investors, they are one and the same person. Learning to balance these divergent but ultimately shared interests is "the challenge of the next 10 years," he said.

Some 45 years ago Drucker declared a celebrated premise. "There is only one valid definition of business purpose: to create a customer." Does that premise still pertain? "What else?" he asked. "Who else pays the bills?" From that conviction has come his creed: Value and service first, profit later. Maximizing profit, perhaps never.

Drucker will turn 90 on Friday. If he lived in Japan (where he has many devoted adherents), he might be denominated a living National Treasure. What he has lost among the business elite as a guru, he has picked up among the public as a civic essayist. For 30 years, he said, he has been writing as much for those who manage the nonprofit world as for those in the corporate ranks.

At latest count, he has written 31 books, most still in print. In his 90th year, he has published a vigorously prescriptive book (*Management Challenges for the 21st Century*, HarperBusiness, 1999), graced *The Atlantic*'s cover and was the featured essayist in *The Economist*'s annual issue on the world economy.

Typically, Drucker gave the global bankers the back of his hand: They have introduced not "a single major innovation in 30 years," he said. Rather, the financial industry has turned inward to perfecting "supposedly 'scientific' derivatives," in a shortsighted hope of wringing the risk out of financial speculation, like Las Vegas gamblers futilely trying to devise "systems" to beat the house.

Drucker's intellectual vitality is breathtaking. His earliest management study, *The Concept of the Corporation*, a scholarly reflection on General Motors, dates back to the Truman presidency. His latest reflections, in the Atlantic cover essay, take aim at the Internet.

Drucker knows how to put a high gloss on things. He writes that only now, with the explosive emergence of e-commerce as a sales channel for goods and services, is "the truly revolutionary impact of the Information Revolution beginning to be felt." Like the railroad at the industrial dawn, e-commerce is "totally new, totally unprecedented, totally unexpected."

In its day, the railroad drastically altered the conception of distance that people carried in their heads. "In the mental geography of e-commerce, distance has been eliminated," Drucker writes. "There is only one economy and only one market." That's a game effort, but "portentous" may be the right word: "full of unspecifiable significance; exciting wonder and awe."

Drucker has been chucking for half a century. Like Orel Hershiser, sometimes the fading champion has his stuff, sometimes he hasn't. Like others in his line of work, Drucker draws lessons from his consulting engagements. He is not above "improving" on the facts to sharpen a point.

Yet nowhere today is there a business prophet as inspirational as Peter Drucker in full stride. This is a man who absorbed management across the desk from Alfred P. Sloan, the General Motors patriarch, who invented the modern corporation. Drucker's widely influential work, *The Practice of Management*, was published during Eisenhower's first term. His opus, *Management: Tasks, Responsibilities, Practices*, became a best seller three decades ago, before OPEC's ascendancy, before the Japanese auto invasion. (Though it deals respectfully with Japan, the 839-page tome does not mention Toyota.)

To young business readers of earlier decades, he seemed a halogen intellect, original and erudite, supremely confident, applying a searchlight to the ordinary routines of business. Though his grand models were Sears, Marks & Spencer, General Motors and IBM, Drucker was capable of a lyrical riff on the nineteenth-century Indian Civil Service, the 1,000 or so young Englishmen who brought order to India in a triumph of middle management. The very quality of his attention elevated management to a calling, "the most important function in American society."

Drucker taught that a manager's success lay in an acute grasp of what the business was really all about, usually a grasp of its contribution to the public good. One hero was Theodore Vail, father of the Bell System, who was unusual among his turn-of-the-century colleagues in concluding that fighting public regulation was a no-win tack. He understood that the phone company's true product was service. The Bell System flourished for more than half a century because it provided that service with a dedication far superior to anything conceivable in a state-owned enterprise.

In the long run, the trademark erudition and the organ music are less lasting than the immense common sense. *The Practice of Management*, pathfinding in its time, now reads musty and antiquarian, with its instructive references to Packard Motor Car Co. But a decade later, in *Managing for Results*, Drucker chiseled a management guide for all seasons.

Results are obtained by exploiting opportunities, not by solving problems. What advice could be hoarier than that? Yet how many established companies have embraced the opportunity of the Internet, rather than feared the threat? Any leadership position is transitory and likely to be short-lived. . . . What exists is getting old. Drucker was already preaching that a successful company must cannibalize its own products, before the competition does. The apostles of our New Economy were yet unborn.

The pertinent question for managers, he wrote, "is not how to do things right but how to find the right things to do." It is pure Drucker: Effectiveness always trumps efficiency. And this was (and is) close to his heart: "The one truly effective way to cut costs is to cut out an activity altogether. There is little point in trying to do cheaply what should not be done at all."

Drucker has kept abreast (or ahead) of the changing tides in business. In 1985, he published *Innovation and Entrepreneurship*, an entirely respectable treatment that by today's IPO standards seems impossibly conservative. In a typical page or so he ropes together 3M Co., the University of Berlin, the Mayo Clinic and the March of Dimes. All that under "Fustest with the Mostest," a strategy the Internet has labeled "first mover advantage."

Today, the deepest pool of Druckerites is undoubtedly in the social sector, a lifelong interest of increasing importance to Drucker. In the nonprofit world, participants openly pursue the greater good. And the social sector—churches, hospitals, schools, community service groups—grows by leaps and bounds. With its woeful management practices, the field was ripe for his intellectual rigor. "I see results," he said in the interview. "The impact is much more direct. They need me more. They start out from so much lower base."

"This is the discipline of innovation," he lectured a convocation of his followers. "It means having a clear mission. It means defining what you mean by results. It means the ability and willingness to abandon where you don't get results. And then when you find the real opportunity, the unique opportunity where you can make the greatest difference, zone in on it, and reassess and reassess and reassess."

Generous with his time and energy, Drucker has devoted a substantial time to pro bono consulting. (Jack Beatty writes in *The World According to Peter*

Drucker that to be taken seriously, he has always charged nonprofits his usual fees, then donated the check.)

Most prominently he serves as guiding light to the Peter F. Drucker Foundation for Nonprofit Management (www.pfdf.org), a group in Manhattan that encourages effective management by recognizing accomplishments by community organizations across the land. Its work is impressively concrete and practical. Most likely it is where we will find Peter Drucker's lasting monument.

The New York Times, November 17, 1999
http://www.nytimes.com/library/jobmarket/111799manage-drucker.html

CRITICAL THINKING QUESTIONS

1. What is the relationship between self-interest and societal interest? Can managers pursue their own self-interest and at the same time benefit society? If so, how? If not, why not?
2. Beyond wages, salary and the other customary benefits, what—if anything—does management owe employees?
3. Should managers concentrate their efforts on enhancing a company's bottom line or on the company's obligation to society?

STORY-SPECIFIC QUESTIONS

1. How many years has it been since the corporate heavy hitters fell on Peter Drucker's every word?
2. Some 45 years ago Drucker declared a celebrated premise. How did he define the purpose of business?
3. What was Drucker's single most important contribution to management?
4. According to Drucker, what is the most pertinent question for management?
5. Why has Drucker become disillusioned with current management practices?

SHORT APPLICATION ASSIGNMENTS

1. In teams or individually, answer the story-specific questions; keep your answers to 25–75 words for each question.
2. In teams of three to five persons, or as a whole class, discuss your responses to the critical thinking questions.
3. Prepare a one-page memo report (200–250 words) to your instructor in which you summarize this article. You will find a model one-page report on the Web site (nytimes.swcollege.com).
4. Write an executive summary (200–250 words). As an administrative assistant to a busy executive, you are expected to summarize selected articles and present important points. You will find a model executive summary on the Web site.

5. Summarize this article (100–125 words) for your company's newsletter. You will find a model newsletter article on the Web site.
6. Peter Drucker now serves "as the guiding light" to the Peter F. Drucker Foundation for Nonprofit Management. Visit the Web site (www.pfdf.org). What is the purpose of the Foundation? What has it accomplished? Prepare an overview (250–500 words) of the Foundation.

BUILDING RESEARCH SKILLS

1. Read Michael Lewis's review (www.nytimes.com/books/98/01/11/reviews/980111. 11lewist.html) of *The World According to Peter Drucker*, by Jack Beatty as well as the book itself. How do the review and book portray Drucker? What additional insights do they offer into his life and management style? Your instructor may ask you to submit a three- to five-page essay, post a Web page or report your results in a five-minute presentation, along with a letter of transmittal explaining your findings.
2. *The Concept of the Corporation* is a classic Peter Drucker book. What are the central tenets of this book? How have managers adopted his prescriptions? Your instructor may ask you to submit a three- to five-page essay, post a Web page or report your results in a five-minute presentation, along with a letter of transmittal explaining your findings.
3. Using at least three other references (e.g., books, research-journal articles, newspaper or magazine stories or credible Web sites), post an 800- to 1,000-word Web page that addresses two of the earlier critical thinking questions. Assume that your Web page will be used as an internal reference for a corporation's intranet.
4. Using at least three other references (e.g., books, research-journal articles, newspaper or magazine stories or credible Web sites), write an 800- to 1,000-word essay that addresses two of the earlier critical thinking questions. Assume that your essay will be used as an internal reference for a corporation's business plan.

Science Squints at a Future Fogged by Chaotic Uncertainty

By Malcolm W. Browne

Back during China's Shang dynasty, around 3,500 years ago, sages foretold the future by casting oracle bones—the clairvoyant equivalent of crap shooting.

Things have changed somewhat since then, even though predictions are as much in demand as ever, and even though we still send plenty of business to astrologers, tarot-card readers, numerologists, phrenologists, necromancers and psychics of all stripes. Aside from the traditional soothsayers, we sometimes also heed forecasts based on observations, scientific synthesis and reasoning.

Scientific sages depend not on tea leaves or the positions of planets but on tools like mathematical modeling, statistical analysis, complexity theory, celestial mechanics, geology, economics and epidemiology. Needless to say, scientists discount the naïve paradigms of fortune tellers, ancient and modern.

Alas, rational approaches to prediction also fail all too often, and it may be that there are some phenomena for which predictions will remain forever out of reach.

As the stock market lurches between the tugs of bulls and bears, financial analysts armed with statistics and the latest marketing theories throw up their hands in despair when asked to guess what will happen from one day to the next.

Picnic planners know better than to rely on short-term weather forecasts, and meteorologists offer little hope that truly accurate weather predictions for specific places and times will ever be possible.

Relief agencies get little useful help from experts as they try to brace for disasters that might, with equal likelihood, occur tomorrow or a thousand years from now. Understanding the mechanisms of events like earthquakes and volcanoes offers little help in predicting precisely when they will occur.

Geologists have a pretty good idea that earthquakes are caused by the movement of tectonic plates, yet the art of earthquake forecasting remains notoriously imprecise.

The largest earthquake in four years—an 8.2-magnitude tremor centered under the ocean between Australia and Antarctica—caught seismologists completely off guard when it shook the sea floor last March 25, and geologists are still puzzled by the quake; it did not occur at the junction of tectonic plates where most quakes occur, but struck within a single plate.

Future seismic surprises, including those causing catastrophic loss of life, seem inevitable.

The tsunami that roared over Papua New Guinea on July 17, killing more than 2,000 people, caught everyone by surprise. Experts excused their failure to warn the population on the ground that a giant tsunami wave materializes only when a scarcely noticeable wave spawned by an earthquake or some other event far out at sea reaches shallow coastal water. By then it is almost on top of some hapless coast line, leaving no time to prepare.

There have been recent reminders that even in principle, some things are impossible to predict.

Among the puzzles that have perplexed mathematicians and physicists at least since the time of Isaac Newton in the seventeenth century is the "N-body problem" (sometimes called the "Many-body problem").

One of Newton's monumental discoveries was that any two objects attract each other with a force proportional to their masses and inversely proportional to the square of their distance apart. But when three or more objects—the Sun, the Earth and the Moon, for example—are interacting gravitationally, exact solutions of the equations describing their motions generally remain beyond reach.

Fortunately, since Newton's day, some very good approximate solutions of N-body equations have been devised, and such solutions have allowed space scientists to send vehicles to the distant reaches of the solar system with astounding precision.

This month, Dr. Gregory R. Buck of Saint Anselm College, in Manchester, New Hampshire, disclosed a new class of approximate N-body solutions based on the analogy of a closed loop of beads, in which the beads, evenly spaced, chase each other around the curves and tangles of the loop. The system may help to work out the interactions of particles within a plasma, Buck suggested.

But none of the approximations now known exactly solve Newton's equations, and this means that the motions of asteroids and comets can be predicted only up to a certain point in the distant future. Beyond that, forecasting an impact by one of these objects on the earth may be intrinsically impossible. A hit or miss may depend so sensitively on the minuscule "initial conditions" of all the objects involved that precise calculation becomes impossible. This is a property of a large class of systems scientists describe as chaotic.

Long-term foreknowledge of the hit or miss—a question of life or death for millions—is ruled out by the chaos inherent in the N-body system.

Scientists have yet to come to terms with chaos in all its manifestations. Dr. Steven Weinberg, winner of a Nobel prize in physics, once said he considered an understanding of chaotic turbulence in fluids as the single most intractable problem in physics. Until scientists reach a deeper understanding of turbulence, many physicists believe, the dynamics of climate change, the behavior of galaxies and many other phenomena can never be fully penetrated.

Chaos can also prevent reliable predictions of group decisions, including those that investors make. Group decisions by investors can cause chaotic price fluctuations of commodities that are intrinsically unpredictable, it seems.

Malcolm W. Browne

In a report published August 24 in the journal *Physical Review Letters*, Dr. David A. Meyer of the University of California at San Diego and Dr. Thad A. Brown of the University of Missouri presented formal proof that collective decisions can be chaotic, even when the views of all participants are known and a standard voting rule is strictly applied.

When a group of decision-makers must choose between three or more options by comparing two of them at a time, the collective outcome often depends on the order in which the choices are presented. The outcome can cycle chaotically, the mathematicians found. Even nonhuman decision-makers—the computers that buy and sell commodities according to programmed rules, for example—are subject to chaotic uncertainty, a situation in which prediction becomes impossible.

Frustrated by the complex and chaotic behavior of the real world, some theorists have invented forecasting techniques based on little more than pure mathematics.

In the 1970s, René Thom, a French mathematician, developed an approach called Catastrophe Theory, which, for a time, enjoyed a considerable vogue among physicists, biologists and even sociologists. The theory is an application of topology, a field of mathematics that deals with the shapes of surfaces.

Thom's theory holds that many sequences of events can be represented as smooth trajectories along a saddle-shaped surface, at one point of which an abrupt discontinuity, or "catastrophe cusp," shunts them off to one side of the saddle or the other.

Thom and his followers proposed that mathematical models based on catastrophe cusps could be used to predict the reproduction of bacteria, the behavior of the stock market, heart attacks, biological evolution and the outbreak of war, among many other things. To some, Thom's theory seemed to offer an explanation of almost everything, but many others condemned it as useless. Today, Catastrophe Theory is all but forgotten.

Predicting life spans in the absence of detailed knowledge has long interested scientists as well as insurance statisticians. A forecast of life expectancy based on the average age at death of a person's four grandparents is a simple example of statistical forecasting. But a much more daring approach was devised a few years ago by Dr. J. Richard Gott 3d, a professor of astrophysics at Princeton University.

Gott's scheme is based on the "Copernican principle," which assumes that the odds are overwhelmingly against any particular place or time being "special." From this, Gott reasoned that the mere knowledge of how long something (or someone) has been around is sufficient to estimate how much longer it could last. Based on this system, and the assumption that Homo sapiens appeared on earth about 200,000 years ago, Gott calculated that intelligent human beings are 95-percent certain to survive a minimum of 5,128 years more, and a maximum of 7.8 million years more.

There are those who contend that predictions like these are so vague that they are scarcely more useful than the prophecies of the Delphic oracle in ancient Greece, which was consulted by Socrates, Oedipus and other luminaries of the day. The oracle (operated by a concealed priest or priestess) was so ambiguous it could nearly never be proved wrong.

Scientists will never be able to answer all our questions about future events or to satisfy a deep-seated human yearning to foresee what's coming at us. Some scientific efforts at prediction will always be defeated by the nature of Nature.

Mystic oracles have never shed light on future events either, but even 1,398 years after Socrates' suicide, legions of people continue to visit palmists, astrologists and psychics. It's human to prefer something to nothing at all.

The New York Times, September 22, 1998
http://www.nytimes.com/library/national/science/092298sci-essay.html

CRITICAL THINKING QUESTIONS

1. Given scientific advances, why do so many individuals turn to astrologers, tarot card readers and mystics for solutions to everyday problems?
2. Managers have to confront many situations, many of which are out of their control. Having read the article on chaotic uncertainty, what advice would you offer them? What approach should they take to the problems of everyday management?
3. Although chaos theory may have merit, what are the potential problems if it were applied to management? What are the possible benefits?

STORY-SPECIFIC QUESTIONS

1. "Alas rational approaches to prediction fail all too often." Cite at least two examples from the article.
2. How might chaos theory affect management decision-making?
3. What does the article suggest about our ability to predict the future?

SHORT APPLICATION ASSIGNMENTS

1. In teams or individually, answer the story-specific questions; keep your answers to 25–75 words for each question.
2. In teams of three to five persons, or as a whole class, discuss your responses to the critical thinking questions.
3. Prepare a one-page memo report (200–250 words) to your instructor in which you summarize this article. You will find a model one-page report on the Web site (nytimes.swcollege.com).
4. Write an executive summary (200–250 words). As an administrative assistant to a busy executive, you are expected to summarize selected articles and present important points. You will find a model executive summary on the Web site.

5. What do the proponents of chaos theory have to offer management? How would chaos theory relate to the failure of the "Purple Moon" described in Chapter 1? Your instructor may ask you to present your findings in an oral report or submit a 250- to 300-word summary.

6. As a manager, if you were to apply two concepts from chaos theory to your management practices, what would they be? Your instructor may ask you to present your findings in an oral report or submit a 250- to 300-word summary.

BUILDING RESEARCH SKILLS

1. Chaos theory has been acclaimed by scholars as a "break-through." Margaret J. Wheately is often cited as one of the pre-eminent scholars in the application chaos theory to management. Review her book, *Leadership and the New Science*. Your instructor may ask you to submit a three- to five-page essay, post a Web page or report your results in a five-minute presentation, along with a letter of transmittal explaining why her work is considered a seminal text.

2. Some would argue that chaos theory has little to offer managers in terms of the day-to-day realities they face. Using at least three other references (e.g., books, research-journal articles, newspaper or magazine stories or credible Web sites), support this viewpoint or argue against it in an essay (700–1,000 words) or class presentation (15 minutes or less).

3. Using at least three other references (e.g., books, research-journal articles, newspaper or magazine stories or credible Web sites), post an 800- to 1,000-word Web page that addresses two of the earlier critical thinking questions. Assume that your Web page will be used as an internal reference for a corporation's intranet.

4. Using at least three other references (e.g., books, research-journal articles, newspaper or magazine stories or credible Web sites), write an 800- to 1,000-word essay that addresses two of the earlier critical thinking questions. Assume that your essay will be used as an internal reference for a corporation's business plan.

Applying Complexity Theory to Business Management

By Steve Ditlea

I t's too early to tell if complexity theory—the study of mathematical and computational principles of orderliness and self-organization in nature—will ever become dominant in the management of business. Yet lessons derived by observing adaptive systems, from the unicellular to the global, are altering how executives view their organizations, allocate resources, even know what's knowable about the future of their enterprises.

Trendy phrases like "thriving on chaos," "business ecologies" and "bottom-up organization," with their origins in the now decades-old discoveries of complexity theory, have already entered management discourse, but practical applications have taken longer to emerge.

The quest for such applications is bringing together top scientists from a wide range of disciplines and top executives from a variety of industries for a set of two conferences, titled Complexity & Technology: Organizing for Innovation, to examine how complexity theory can be applied to business.

According to a Web site for the conferences—being held on Thursday and Friday in Phoenix, Arizona, and on March 10 and 11 in London—they will be aimed at "senior executives and managers who have major strategic, operational or management responsibilities."

Actually, anyone with $2,200 (or £1,500) to spare can attend the presentations by an all-star line-up of complexity theorists. And despite the meetings' erudite title, you don't have to be a technology whiz to appreciate them.

"This is not science," insisted Mike McMaster, the organizer and co-chairman of the conferences and a speaker at both meetings. "This is the philosophy and art of management."

Confessing to little knowledge of the computer modeling technology that made possible many of the discoveries of orderliness in nature's seemingly chaotic systems, McMaster prefers to deal in practical metaphors. "Complexity gives us useful conceptual models for business processes that take into account patterns rather than rules," he said.

An example of the new management vocabulary is "attractors," the term for theoretical points around which complex patterns can organize themselves, setting boundaries amid the apparently chaotic pull of countless variables. Whether the subject is weather or economic fluctuations, attractors influence great forces with no apparent effort.

"It's an approach to thinking about organizations that's less rigid, more demanding of intelligence," McMaster said.

If all this sounds a bit abstract, the clients of McMaster's London-based consulting firm, Knowledge Based Development, are decidedly down to earth. They include Monsanto, Unilever and BP Exploration.

Among the converted is Colin Crook, senior vice president for technology at Citicorp in New York and one of the speakers at the London conference. Applications of complexity theory to Citicorp's operations, he said, have exceeded expectations. He added, "We are surprised and delighted by the measurable results."

While shunning details for competitive reasons, Crook cited general areas of research that have benefited Citicorp, including predicting consumer credit behavior and personal bankruptcies.

To put complexity to use, in 1995 Citicorp helped set up the Center for Adaptive Systems Applications as a spin-off of the Los Alamos National Laboratory, where nonlinear adaptive computation—i.e., high-speed modeling of complex situations with a supercomputer—had been applied to commercial problems like chemical-process control, fraud detection in financial flows and scheduling for large processing centers.

Among the valuable organizational lessons learned, Crook said, was "that a lot of long-range planning doesn't make sense."

"The three- to five-year forecasts that most financial institutions do can't possibly be accurate, given all the variables," he said. "At Citicorp, now we only do six-quarter rolling forecasts."

As executives reexamine the working assumptions behind their enterprises, proponents of complexity theory say it can provide answers for questions that current business theory cannot resolve.

Stuart Kauffman, a pioneer of complexity theory and a recipient of a MacArthur Foundation "genius" grant, declared: "Traditional economics can't explain growth in new goods and services. With complex adaptive systems, you can model economic growth driven by growing economic diversity."

Derived from patterns of the evolution of new species of plant and animal life from previous species, these economic models can account for "fitness plateaus"—market niches in which novel goods and services may thrive.

A biologist by training, the garrulous Kauffman (his Complexity & Technology presentations are simply titled "Stu's View of the World") now offers consulting services to businesses through Bios LP, his joint venture with Ernst & Young. The recent startup's clients already include Northern Telecom and the United States Marine Corps. Like many of the leading lights in complexity theory (and like many speakers at the upcoming conferences), Kauffman is affiliated with the Santa Fe Institute, a bastion of multidisciplinary research.

The institute is also home to the Business Network for Complex Systems Research, where management professionals can study the evolution of complex systems displaying "emergent behavior"—that is, activities that could not be predicted from the systems' parts. (The Santa Fe Institute is not affiliated with The Santa Fe Group consulting firm, which is a co-sponsor of the Complexity and Technology conferences).

For another professor at the Santa Fe Institute, the Nobel physics laureate Murray Gell-Mann, emergence means that executives must widen their perspective and take "A Crude Look at the Whole," as his talk in Phoenix is titled.

"Management is dealing with systems such that examining the parts does not give a picture of the whole," Gell-Mann said. "Yet the activities that are rewarded in business are those that encourage a narrow focus and specialization." In rethinking priorities, he added, "as a society, we need to look at the whole and respect that activity not just in an executive, but in all people."

To illustrate his point, Gell-Mann recalled a recent conversation with the chief executive of a large conglomerate: "He said there were just three problems with the people in his strategic planning department—they spoke completely differently from everyone else in the company; nobody could understand them, and everyone started to hate them." Such short-circuiting of useful feedback can only add to the perturbations a large corporation faces in responding to global competition and new information technologies.

In his London presentation, John Seely Brown, the Xerox Corporation's chief scientist and director of the company's legendary Palo Alto Research Center, will discuss "Using the Web as a Medium for Innovation," based on his company's recent experiments in corporate communications.

In Brown's paradigm, "any organization has two components—the 'authorized' and the 'emergent.'" The authorized corresponds to traditional top-down management, while the emergent is the bottom-up input from what he calls "communities of practice," where innovation may originate but not always find its way back to management.

At Xerox, first in France using the Minitel system and more recently in the United States and Canada, the technicians who go out and fix Xerox office equipment have been posting service tips to mediated Web pages on which suggestions are evaluated and often made immediately available to other technicians. As feedback from the technician ranks is evaluated, Xerox management can identify the market environments in which individual models have found a fitness plateau.

"Rural or city, small or large office, we can explore a combinatorial space along eight different dimensions," Brown said. The goal of such efforts using the Web's increasingly familiar hypertext interface, he said, is "to let the small efforts of the many complement the large efforts of the few."

CyberTimes, The New York Times on the Web, February 13, 1997
http://www.nytimes.com/library/cyber/week/021397complex.html

CRITICAL THINKING QUESTIONS

1. Is complexity theory more science than art and philosophy? Why, or why not?
2. Complexity theory offers an alternative world view. In your estimation, can it help managers or is it merely another management trend?
3. Is the whole greater than the sum of the parts? Why, or why not? To honor this adage what must managers do differently? If you were to focus on the whole, on what would you focus? How does one examine an organizational system?

STORY-SPECIFIC QUESTIONS

1. The article suggests that organizations have two components. What are they?
2. List two ways that Xerox used the concepts presented in the article.
3. According to Gell-Mann what problems were associated with the strategic planning departments?
4. The article suggests that strategic planning may be a misguided effort. Why?

SHORT APPLICATION ASSIGNMENTS

1. In teams or individually, answer the story-specific questions; keep your answers to 25–75 words for each question.
2. In teams of three to five persons, or as a whole class, discuss your responses to the critical thinking questions.
3. Prepare a one-page memo report (200–250 words) to your instructor in which you summarize this article. You will find a model one-page report on the Web site (nytimes.swcollege.com).
4. Write an executive summary (200–250 words). As an administrative assistant to a busy executive, you are expected to summarize selected articles and present important points. You will find a model executive summary on the Web site.
5. Summarize this article (100–125 words) for your company's newsletter. You will find a model newsletter article on the Web site.

BUILDING RESEARCH SKILLS

1. Individually or in teams, investigate two of the Web sites mentioned in the article in order to summarize how you could use complexity theory to create a more productive workplace. Your instructor may ask you to submit a three- to five-page essay, post a Web page or report your results in a five-minute presentation, along with a letter of transmittal explaining your findings.
2. Using at least three other references (e.g., books, research-journal articles, newspaper or magazine stories or credible Web sites), write an 800- to 1,000-word essay explaining how "complexity theory" could enhance an organization. Assume that your essay will be used as an internal reference for a corporation's human resources department.

3. Using at least three other references (e.g., books, research-journal articles, news-paper or magazine stories or credible Web sites), post an 800- to 1,000-word Web page that addresses two of the earlier critical thinking questions. Assume that your Web page will be used as an internal reference for a corporation's intranet.

4. Using at least three other references (e.g., books, research-journal articles, news-paper or magazine stories or credible Web sites), write an 800- to 1,000-word essay that addresses two of the earlier critical thinking questions. Assume that your essay will be used as an internal reference for a corporation's business plan.

Leadership

PREVIEW

What makes an effective leader? Historians, philosophers and now management theorists have all asked that question. And the answers are myriad. We recognize and celebrate leadership, but it is difficult to define—let alone teach. Leadership is more than formulas, rules and procedures; personal qualities also influence a leader's success.

Soon after the World War II, the label "Made in Japan" was synonymous with consumer products that were considered to be little more than junk, but not anymore. Today, Japan is synonymous with quality. As Andrew Pollack describes in an obituary, "Akio Morita, Key to Japan's Rise as Co-Founder of Sony, Dies at 78," Akio Morita was in many way responsible for transforming a company and in some ways, a country. A crusader for quality, Morita "personified Japan's rise from postwar rubble to industrial riches."

Like Morita, Oprah Winfrey has the gift of leadership. Smart and charming, she shares her personal leadership thoughts in a course she teaches. Bill Dedman reports on the demand for and content in Winfrey's course in "Professor Oprah, Preaching What She Practices."

Finally, the article "Taking Risks and Allowing Failures" is a partial transcript of a roundtable discussion on leadership. Four chief executives—Larry Bossidy of Allied Signal, Dennis Kozlowski of Tyco International, Charles Wang of Computer Associates International and Shelly Lazarus of Ogilvy & Mather Worldwide—gathered over coffee at the *New York Times* to talk about leadership and how they do their jobs.

The Panel. Left to right are: Charles Wang of Computer Associates; Lawrence A. Bossidy of Allied Signal; Shelley Lazarus of Ogilvy Mather; Dennis Kozlowski of Tyco International.

Source: Angel Franco/The New York Times

Akio Morita, Key to Japan's Rise as Co-Founder of Sony, Dies at 78

By Andrew Pollack

Akio Morita, the co-founder of the Sony Corporation who personified Japan's rise from postwar rubble to industrial riches and became the unofficial ambassador of its business community to the world, died on Sunday in Tokyo. He was 78.

Morita died of pneumonia, according to Sony. He had been hospitalized in Tokyo since August, after returning from Hawaii, where he had spent most of his time since suffering a debilitating stroke in November 1993.

More than anyone else, it was Morita and his Sony colleagues who changed the world's image of the term "Made in Japan" from one of paper parasols and shoddy imitations to one of high technology and high reliability in miniature packages.

Founded in a bombed-out Tokyo department store after World War II, Sony became indisputably one of the world's most innovative companies, famous for products like the pocket-sized transistor radio, the videocassette recorder, the Walkman and the compact disk.

And Morita, whose contribution was greater in marketing than in technology, made the Sony brand into one of the best known and most respected in the world. A Harris poll last year showed Sony was the number one brand name among American consumers, ahead of American companies like General Electric and Coca-Cola.

A tireless traveler who moved his family to New York in 1963 for a year to learn American ways, Morita also spearheaded the internationalization of Japanese business. Sony was the first Japanese company to offer its stock in the United States, in 1961, one of the first to build a factory in the United States, in 1972, and still one of the only ones to have even a couple of Westerners on its board.

Sony also became a major force in the American entertainment business, acquiring CBS Records in 1988 and Columbia Pictures, the Hollywood studio, in 1989.

The latter purchase, however, turned into an embarrassing debacle as Sony suffered big losses in Hollywood.

A JAPANESE EXECUTIVE AMERICANS RECOGNIZED

In the process, Morita, with his white mane and quick tongue, became the unofficial representative of Japan's business community, generally working to

Andrew Pollack

smooth trade relations between his country and the United States, but sometimes stirring resentment in both countries with his pointed criticisms.

"He was truly a statesman par excellence in a business sense," said Mike Mansfield, the former senator and United States Ambassador to Japan. "Internationally, he did more for Japan in a business sense than anyone else in Japan."

In Japan, Prime Minister Keizo Obuchi, who was one of several hundred people to visit Morita's Tokyo home following his death, called Morita "a leading figure who played a pivotal role in developing Japan's postwar economy," according to Kyodo News Service.

Sony's current president, Nobuyuki Idei, said in a statement, "It is not an exaggeration to say that he was the face of Japan."

To the day of his death, nearly six years after the stroke that removed him from an active role in business, he was still no doubt Japan's most famous business executive, and the only one many Americans could name or recognize in a photograph. *Time* magazine recently selected him as one of 20 "most influential business geniuses" of the twentieth century, the only non-American on the list.

In his own country, where executives tend to be self-effacing, Morita was viewed as a bit flamboyant and arrogant. He was the first to fly around in a corporate business jet and helicopter. He appeared in a television commercial for the American Express card. He served on the boards of three foreign companies. He took up sports like skiing, scuba diving and wind surfing in his sixties. He cavorted with the rock star Cyndi Lauper after Sony bought CBS Records.

Shortly before he suffered his stroke, Morita made waves in his home country by saying that Japan was like a "fortress" and that its unique business practices were alienating its trading partners. "Although there is much to commend in Japan's economic system, it is simply too far out of sync with the West on certain essential points," he wrote in *The Atlantic Monthly* in June 1993.

He advocated shorter working hours, more dividends for stockholders of Japanese companies and a sharp cutback in government regulation. Now, as Japan struggles through an economic slump that has lasted most of the decade, some of what Morita advocated is being adopted.

"Japan was coming closer to him and seeing the need for that kind of leadership," said Yoshihiro Tsurumi, professor of international business at the Baruch Graduate School of Business at the City University of New York.

NEVER COMFORTABLE IN WEST'S BUSINESS WORLD

Morita entertained frequently and counted many American businessmen and politicians as his friends. "He not only made it Sony's business but his own personal business to become intimately acquainted with American society at all levels," said Peter Peterson, an investment banker who is on Sony's board of directors. "I can recall playing golf with Akio, watching him greet and interact with every American CEO on the course, all of whom seemed to know him as a personal friend."

In his book *Sony: The Private Life* (Houghton Mifflin, 1999), John Nathan suggests that Morita, a Japanese traditionalist at home, was never really comfortable in the Western business world.

Nathan, a Japanese translator and University of California professor of Japanese culture who was granted free access to Sony executives, quotes Morita's eldest son, Hideo, as saying of his father, "He had to 'act'—I'm sorry to use that word but I can't help it—he had to act as the most international-understanding businessman in Japan." But, Hideo adds, "It was never real."

And Sony's current president, Idei, is quoted as saying: "Japanese of the generation before mine had an inferiority complex about foreigners. Akio Morita himself was a living inferiority complex."

Despite being virtually synonymous with Sony, especially outside Japan, Morita did not actually become the company's president until 1971 and its chairman and chief executive until 1976. Before that, he was the junior partner to Masaru Ibuka, an engineering genius who, while not as widely known in the West, is considered in Japan to be the main founder of Sony. Ibuka died in December 1997 at the age of 89.

AN EARLY FASCINATION LEADS TO A CAREER SHIFT

Akio Morita was born on January 26, 1921, into a wealthy family in Nagoya, an industrial city in central Japan. As the eldest son, he was groomed from elementary school age to succeed his father as president of the sake brewery that had been in the family for 14 generations.

But in junior high school, Akio became fascinated by his family's phonograph, an appliance rare in Japan at that time. He became an avid electronics hobbyist, building his own crude phonograph and radio receiver. He studied physics at Osaka Imperial University as World War II was starting. Morita enlisted in the Navy under a program that would allow him to do research instead of serving in combat.

It was while developing heat-seeking weapons that Morita first worked with Ibuka, 13 years his senior, who before the war had started an electronic instrument company.

After the war, Ibuka set up a new company in a bombed-out department store in Tokyo, making kits that converted AM radios into short-wave receivers. Morita happened to read a newspaper article about this and contacted his old friend. The next year, when Ibuka wanted to incorporate the company, he asked Morita to join.

Morita, Ibuka and another executive traveled to the Nagoya area to implore Morita's father to release his son from the family business. The elder Morita not only agreed, he also later became a financial backer of the new company, Tokyo

Tsushin Kogyo, or the Tokyo Telecommunications Engineering Corporation, which was inaugurated on May 7, 1946, with an investment of about $500.

The company produced Japan's first reel-to-reel magnetic tape recorder. A few years later it licensed the rights to the transistor from Bell Laboratories, after overcoming resistance from the Ministry of International Trade and Industry. Bell Labs officials warned that the only consumer use would be for hearing aids.

But Sony used them to produce Japan's first transistor radio in 1955. (An American company, Regency, produced the world's first a few months earlier but did not succeed in selling it.) In 1957, Sony came out with what it termed a pocket-sized transistor radio. But the radio was actually a bit too big for most pockets, so Morita had Sony salesmen wear special shirts with extra-large pockets.

There followed the Trinitron television in 1968; the first successful home VCR, the Betamax, in 1975; the Walkman personal stereo in 1979, and the compact disk, developed with Philips N.V. of the Netherlands, in 1982.

Not all products were successful. Sony has stumbled several times trying to sell personal computers. And in 1981, Morita announced the Mavica, a digital camera that recorded pictures on a floppy disk instead of on film. But the camera did not come to market and critics accused Morita of making a premature announcement to burnish Sony's image as an innovator.

STEERING CONSUMERS TO PRODUCTS THEY WANT

Morita did not believe in market research. "Our plan is to lead the public with new products rather than ask them what kind of products they want," he declared in his autobiography, *Made in Japan* (E. P. Dutton, 1986), written with the journalists Edwin M. Reingold and Mitsuko Shimomura. "The public does not know what is possible, but we do."

Morita prided himself in particular on the Walkman, the portable stereo cassette player with headphones. Actually, according to the company's official corporate history, it was Ibuka who came up with the idea for the portable product. But Morita pressed hard for the project, overcoming resistance within Sony to a tape player that, in its early versions, could not record. Morita, despite initial reservations about the awkward name, eventually ordered all Sony subsidiaries around the world to begin using it.

From the start of the company, however, Morita was much more involved in marketing, while Ibuka handled technology development. And from the start, he had an international orientation, traveling to New York and Europe in the 1950s to sell the company wares.

Such international focus was needed because as a new company, Sony had some trouble breaking into its home market, where more established manufacturers had close relationships with retailers. Indeed, Japan's other big postwar success, the Honda Motor Company, also succeeded first in the United States and to this day sells more cars in America than in Japan.

Morita soon realized that the company needed a name that foreigners could pronounce and remember. So in 1958 the company name was changed to Sony, derived from the Latin sonus, meaning sound, and from the American vernacular "sonny boy," which Morita hoped would purvey a young image.

One of Morita's cardinal tenets was to foster and protect the company's brand name. Early on, Bulova, the watch company, said it would order 100,000 radios but would sell them under its own name. Morita turned down the huge order. His colleagues back in Tokyo thought he was crazy. But, Morita wrote in his autobiography, "I said then and I have said it often since: It was the best decision I ever made."

Morita's worst decision might have been with the Betamax, the first successful consumer VCR. Sony did not readily license its technology to other electronics companies. So most of its Japanese rivals banded together behind the VHS system, which offered longer recording time. Eventually, the Betamax was run out of the market.

Sony evolved into a company that, by Japanese standards at least, was very Westernized, though in many ways it was traditionally Japanese. All company employees, from the president on down, wore company jackets, a common practice in Japan. But Sony's uniforms were created by the designer Issey Miyake.

Morita first criticized some of his country's business practices in 1966, when he wrote a book, published in Japanese, with a title that might loosely translate as *An Essay on the Useless School Career*. He criticized Japanese companies for hiring and promoting people based only on what college they had attended. Sony stopped even asking applicants the name of their college, and it was one of the first Japanese companies to base salaries partly on merit instead of solely on seniority.

TRIED TO REDUCE U.S. TRADE TENSIONS

Perhaps because of Sony's dependence on exports, Morita tried to reduce trade tensions with the United States. In the late 1960s, Sony forged a temporary joint venture with Texas Instruments Inc., then the world's leading semiconductor company, allowing it to set up operations in Japan.

In 1972, Morita set up a subsidiary to export American products, like Regal cookware and Whirlpool refrigerators, to Japan.

"Selling pans and cookware and refrigerators was not our bag, but Akio believed in doing something for the U.S.-Japan relationship," said Sadami (Chris) Wada, who ran that effort and then handled government relations for the Sony Corporation of America for many years. The operation was abandoned some years later as unsuccessful.

In 1988, Morita founded the Council for Better Corporate Citizenship, made up of Japanese companies. At a time when Japanese politicians were angering African-Americans with insensitive remarks, one of the council's first projects was to make thousands of copies of an abridged version of "Eyes on the Prize," the American television documentary about the struggle of blacks for equal rights, and distribute it to high schools in Japan.

Morita was not averse to using his influence among American politicians and business executives to lobby for Sony. He barnstormed the United States in 1984, meeting with governors and with President Reagan, threatening to build Sony factories only in states that did not have the "unitary tax," which was levied against a multinational corporation's global earnings, not just those in the state. Eventually California and other states scrapped the tax.

But while Morita was often perceived as a friend of the United States, he was often critical of it and proud of being Japanese, flying his country's flag over Sony's New York showroom when it opened in 1962. He often told a story of how ashamed he was on his first trip to Germany in 1953. At a restaurant, he ordered ice cream, and it was served with a small paper parasol stuck in it. "This is from your country," the waiter said.

HAILING THE SUCCESS OF THE JAPANESE WAY

In the 1980s, when Japan seemed on top of the world, Morita was among the most vocal of the Japanese executives in criticizing American business and hailing the success of the Japanese model.

He said American managers were financial paper shufflers who "can see only 10 minutes ahead" and were not interested in building for the long term. And he said that because American companies were losing interest in manufacturing, the United States was "abandoning its status as an industrial power." Those factors, he said, and not trade barriers, were the reason for America's trade deficit with Japan.

"There are few things in the United States that Japanese want to buy, but there are a lot of things in Japan that Americans want to buy," he wrote in 1989. "This is at the root of the trade imbalance. The problem arises in that American politicians fail to understand this simple fact."

In 1989, Morita was the co-author, along with a nationalist politician, Shintaro Ishihara, of *The Japan That Can Say No*, a book that urged Japan to stand up to American trade demands, which it said were motivated partly by racism. The book also said Japan had the power to change the world balance of power by selling its advanced computer chips to the Soviet Union instead of the United States.

Even though those strident remarks were generally in the chapters Ishihara wrote, the book created a stir when an unauthorized translation made its way around Washington. Morita frantically back-pedaled, saying the book had not been intended for an American audience. And he refused to authorize an English translation.

$3.2 BILLION LOST IN HOLLYWOOD VENTURE

It was later that year that Sony paid $3.4 billion to buy Columbia Pictures, a purchase driven largely by Morita, who thought that if Sony had owned a studio issuing movies in the Beta format, it would not have lost the VCR wars.

Although Sony prided itself on being more Americanized than its Japanese rivals, the purchase became a lightning rod for American concern about a wave of Japanese acquisitions of American companies and real estate. "Japan Invades Hollywood" read the cover of *Newsweek*. In Japan as well, Sony came in for criticism for stirring up anti-Japanese feeling in the United States.

Morita had a simple answer. "If you don't want Japan to buy it, don't sell it," he told a *New York Times* reporter shortly after the purchase. Nevertheless, sensitive to concerns, he promised that the studio would be run by Americans and would be free even to make a movie critical of Japan's emperor.

Worse than misjudging the political reaction, however, the seemingly sophisticated Sony proved to be a babe in the woods in Hollywood.

Sony is generally considered to have overpaid for the studio, and it paid several hundred million dollars more to hire managers away from Warner Brothers—provoking a costly fight with that studio. Those managers, in turn, spent money extravagantly and produced a string of box office bombs. Morita and his successor as Sony chief executive, Norio Ohga, perhaps because they were worried about stirring up anti-Japanese sentiment, exercised little oversight.

In late 1994, in one of the most embarrassing moments in its history, Sony announced that it would suffer a loss of $3.2 billion from its investment in Hollywood. But it has stuck with the studio, now called Sony Pictures Entertainment, and appears to be turning it around.

The Morita name will live on at Sony because many members of Morita's family are involved in the company.

Besides his wife, Morita is survived by his wife, Yoshiko; his eldest son, Hideo, who now runs the sake brewery and other family businesses; a younger son, Masao, an executive with Sony Music Entertainment in Japan; and a daughter, Naoko Okada, who also lives in Japan. He is also survived by his brother Kazuaki, who volunteered to take over the family sake brewery in Morita's stead; another brother, Masaaki, a long-time Sony executive, and a sister, Kikuko Iwama, who was married to the late Kazuo Iwama, a former president of Sony.

A LONGTIME OUTSIDER IS EMBRACED AT LAST

In the 1990s, corporate Japan, worried about escalating trade tensions, turned to Morita, whom it once considered an arrogant maverick, to be its official leader. Morita was slated to become chairman of Keidanren, Japan's most powerful business lobbying organization, a post that had always gone to the head of a company in an old-line heavy industry like steel.

But on November 30, 1993, while playing his usual 7 A.M. Tuesday tennis game, Morita suffered a cerebral hemorrhage. A year later, just days after Sony announced its huge Hollywood loss, Morita, in a wheelchair, attended a Sony board meeting in Tokyo and resigned as chairman.

He had spent much of his time since then undergoing rehabilitation at his beachfront home near Diamond Head on the Hawaiian island of Oahu. At first, Morita was able to speak a little, shake hands and hit back tennis balls spit out by a machine, according to Wada, the retired Sony government relations manager.

But more recently, Wada said, Morita had lost the ability to speak and communicated mainly through eye contact with his wife. The couple's Christmas greeting card last year had a message from Mrs. Morita saying her husband rose at 6 A.M., retired at 9 P.M. and spent much of the day in rehabilitation. "He may be overeating," she said, mentioning his fondness for eel.

Until he was taken to the hospital in Tokyo in August, Morita had not returned to Japan for more than two years because of concerns that flying would further damage his health. He did not attend the 1997 funeral of Ibuka.

But Sony officials still visited him in Hawaii to keep him up to date on the business and show him new products. In January 1998, some 200 executives, friends and dignitaries came to Hawaii to attend a party for Morita's 77th birthday, considered a lucky age in Japan.

The New York Times, October 3, 1999
http://www.nytimes.com/library/world/asia/100399obit-morita.html

CRITICAL THINKING QUESTIONS

1. What were the personal characteristics that made Akio Morita a leader? Why were these characteristics important?
2. Morita gave a new meaning to the phrase "Made in Japan." What management practices helped him establish Sony as one of the most respected companies in the world and transform the world's perception of Japanese products? Why did these practices help?
3. Morita had a vision for not only his company, but for Japan. In your estimation, what was that vision?

STORY-SPECIFIC QUESTIONS

1. Akio Morita remarked that Japan was a fortress and that its business practices were alienating its trading partners. What did Morita advocate changing?
2. List two efforts that Morita initiated to reduce trade tensions with the United States.
3. What was Morita's opinion of market research?

4. Morita is credited with making his company's name a household word. List two steps he took to promote the name.
5. Despite his appreciation for the West, Morita also was a critic of American management. What were two of his criticisms?

SHORT APPLICATION ASSIGNMENTS

1. In teams or individually, answer the story-specific questions; keep your answers to 25–75 words for each question.
2. In teams of three to five persons, or as a whole class, discuss your responses to the critical thinking questions.
3. Prepare a one-page memo report (200–250 words) to your instructor in which you summarize this article. You will find a model one-page report on the Web site (nytimes.swcollege.com).
4. Write an executive summary (200–250 words). As an administrative assistant to a busy executive, you are expected to summarize selected articles and present important points. You will find a model executive summary on the Web site.
5. Summarize this article (100–125 words) for your company's newsletter. You will find a model newsletter article on the Web site.

BUILDING RESEARCH SKILLS

1. Using at least two resources and Sony's Web site (www.sony.com), research the status of Sony since Akio Morita's death. For example, who is the current CEO/President of Sony? Have the fortunes of Sony Pictures Entertainment been turned around? What are the new products that Sony is promoting? What do Sony's latest financial reports show? Your instructor may ask you to submit a three- to five-page essay, post a Web page or report your results in a five-minute presentation, along with a letter of transmittal explaining your results.
2. Japan has struggled through an economic slump that has lasted most of the decade. What is the current economic status of Japan's economy? Has it recovered from its recession? What steps has the government taken to promote economic growth? Your instructor may ask you to submit a three- to five-page essay, post a Web page or report your results in a five-minute presentation, along with a letter of transmittal explaining your results.
3. Write a 400- to 600-word biography of Morita's life. For more information on Morita, see John Nathan's *Sony: The Private Life* or other library sources. What did you learn about him that was not included in the text?
4. Using at least three other references (e.g., books, research-journal articles, newspaper or magazine stories or credible Web sites), post an 800- to 1,000-word Web page that addresses two of the earlier critical thinking questions. Assume that your Web page will be used as an internal reference for a corporation's intranet.
5. Using at least three other references (e.g., books, research-journal articles, newspaper or magazine stories or credible Web sites), write an 800- to 1,000-word essay that addresses two of the earlier critical thinking questions. Assume that your essay will be used as an internal reference for a corporation's business plan.

Professor Oprah, Preaching What She Practices

By Bill Dedman

Evanston, Illinois—At Northwestern University's Kellogg Graduate School of Management here, course registration is a study in perfect competition. To select courses, MBA students bid against one another. Each starts with the same number of points; courses with popular professors cost more.

The bidding this fall was especially nerve-wracking for Walter D. Scott, a professor of management. On Monday nights, he teaches a course in leadership.

The Tuesday night class in leadership is taught by Oprah Winfrey.

"I was a little bit concerned over the summer, to say the least, that I would end up with no students," Scott said.

Some students bid 2,800 points—out of 3,000 points for the entire year—to win one of the 110 seats in Ms. Winfrey's course, "Dynamics of Leadership." For the rest of the school year, they were willing to take a seat wherever they could find one.

When Northwestern announced in May that it had hired a talk show host as a part-time professor, for at least this one-term experiment, faculty members began receiving derisive e-mails from peers at other B-schools. Would the students sit in warm baths, surrounded by candles? Would a blackboard chart of positive externalities involve weight loss?

Doubts among the Kellogg professors deepened. "The initial reaction from everyone was, 'Huh? What's all that about?'" Scott said. "There was a genuine concern that the sensationalization may not be good for the institution."

The dean, Donald P. Jacobs, assured them that he had hired Ms. Winfrey, despite her lack of scholarly credentials, because of her entrepreneurial ones. (She has a degree in speech communications and theater from Tennessee State University.) Through the Chicago offices of her Harpo Entertainment Group, she is involved in television, film, video, publishing, philanthropy, the Internet, education and health and fitness.

Still to come are a magazine and cable channel for women. She ranks 348th on the *Forbes* magazine list of the wealthiest Americans, with an estimated net worth of $725 million. She is the highest ranking woman who didn't inherit at least part of her fortune.

Northwestern's B-school is ranked among the top three by *Business Week* and *U.S. News & World Report*, although its own professors are known for teaching marketing more than entrepreneurship. So who better to add to the faculty?

"Students get the best woman in business, and the best entrepreneurial female in the world," said Richard P. Honack, an assistant dean and associate professor of marketing.

As an elective, her course is open only to second-year students. Even those who were betting on the new professor weren't sure what to expect. "Part of it was just the allure of Oprah," said Susan Moseley, 28, of Atlanta, in the class of 2000. "I think everybody expects that this is not going to be your basic business school class."

Others, however, gamely played down celebrity's allure. "I wouldn't ever have taken the course because Professor Winfrey is teaching it," said Jeff Jones, 26, of Louisville. "But she has interacted with great leaders from all fields."

On the first day of class, Ms. Moseley and Jones had to show their IDs to pass through security. No cameras or tape recorders allowed.

"I'm a little nervous about it," Ms. Winfrey told reporters gathered outside. "I was doing my homework last night."

In the classroom, Ms. Winfrey quickly involved students in a discussion, asking each for a synonym for leadership. She let the students make her point: Everyone has a different idea of a leader.

Stressing the course's theme of "personal leadership," Ms. Winfrey pounded two words in the opening class: intention and authentic. She described how her success came from setting goals and focusing on achieving them. And she described the value of having an authentic leadership style that matched one's personality. Leaders, she said, must look inward, admit mistakes and recognize their weaknesses.

"She is funny, down to earth, extremely charismatic," said Ms. Moseley, who has worked in nonprofit marketing and for Intel. "There was a lot of great discussion, a lot of participation, a high level of energy and people were excited to be there."

Jones, who came to Kellogg from the Federal Reserve Bank of St. Louis, found her the opposite of a haughty entertainment star. "I think the thing that impressed me the most was how personable she was," he said. "You would have never known what she did or who she was."

Ms. Winfrey's boyfriend, Stedman Graham—the co-teacher, as though anyone noticed—is a sports marketing executive, author and regular Northwestern lecturer. He leads students through the cases, while Ms. Winfrey speaks more from personal experience.

Students said she hasn't just poured out random war stories, as visiting lecturers are prone to do, but has offered anecdotes and observations to match the cases.

"To some extent, Oprah's role is one of motivation, as an example of somebody who came from extremely humble beginnings and has built an empire," Ms. Moseley said. "It's easier to believe in my possibilities when I'm hearing it from somebody who's built an amazing career from nothing but charisma and hard work."

Students were warned not to share the class syllabus or materials, which Ms. Winfrey said she worked on all summer, with anyone. But the 475-page packet of readings is available for $60.50 at the campus bookstore. The cases come directly from the Harvard Business School, but readings focus more on "self-realization," "realizing intention through action" and "developing your travel plan."

The textbook is *Principle-Centered Leadership*, (Franklin Covey Co., 1990) by the best-selling author Stephen R. Covey.

Each week, as in many Kellogg courses, student teams analyze management cases, in writing. Ms. Winfrey also requires students to keep journals reflecting on the course and their own experiences. Half the grade comes from a final case analysis. "No late papers will be accepted," the syllabus warns.

When the bidding finished, the course cost students just 1,006 of their 3,000 points for the year, because each student pays only the amount bid by the one who takes the last seat. Even that price will fall if any students who wanted only one or two sessions with Ms. Winfrey drop the course and others who bid fewer points take their places.

It could be a bargain. A science-fiction author from Dallas spent $58,750 at a charity auction this month for the privilege of lunch and a yoga class with Ms. Winfrey, along with two backstage passes to her show. For $11,212 less, he could have enrolled in the Kellogg School for a year and sat in the front row of her class every Tuesday evening.

And Scott, who sneaked a peek at Ms. Winfrey's syllabus, is no longer worried about the integrity of the school.

"It looked to me legitimate, substantive, a thoughtful course on leadership," he said. He brings in distinguished executives to expose the students to various styles of leadership, but he recognizes that Ms. Winfrey fills that role herself.

"She is a practitioner, and this is one of those fields where the state of the art may be more with the practitioner than with the academic," he said. "I think she brings a great deal to the party."

Of course, he said, "It's easier for me to say that now. My class has a wait list."

The New York Times, October 10, 1999
http://www.nytimes.com/library/financial/sunday/101099personal-oprah.html

CRITICAL THINKING QUESTIONS

1. Define what it means to be an effective leader. Justify your opinion with examples of outstanding management leaders.
2. What makes an enduring leader? Why are some individuals considered great leaders only to be forgotten by history?
3. If you were to select one individual to teach a course in management leadership, who would you select? Why?

STORY-SPECIFIC QUESTIONS

1. How did the dean and the assistant dean justify hiring Oprah Winfrey?
2. One of the Northwestern professors ultimately came to Ms. Winfrey's defense. How did he describe her contribution?
3. What were the two words (concepts) that Ms. Winfrey stressed in her opening class?

SHORT APPLICATION ASSIGNMENTS

1. In teams or individually, answer the story-specific questions; keep your answers to 25–75 words for each question.
2. In teams of three to five persons, or as a whole class, discuss your responses to the critical thinking questions.
3. Prepare a one-page memo report (200–250 words) to your instructor in which you summarize this article. You will find a model one-page report on the Web site (nytimes.swcollege.com).
4. Write an executive summary (200–250 words). As an administrative assistant to a busy executive, you are expected to summarize selected articles and present important points. You will find a model executive summary on the Web site.
5. Summarize this article (100–125 words) for your company's newsletter. You will find a model newsletter article on the Web site.
6. Why, in your estimation, did Northwestern hire Ms. Winfrey? What were the pros and the cons of the decision? Prepare an essay (250–500 words) or a presentation (5–10 minutes) that addresses Northwestern's decision.

BUILDING RESEARCH SKILLS

1. Ms. Winfrey selected Stephen Covey's *Principled Centered Leadership* as her course text. Obtain a copy of the book and write a 500- to 1,000-word overview of its central thesis.
2. Using at least three other references (e.g., books, research-journal articles, newspaper or magazine stories or credible Web sites), write an 800- to 1,000-word word biography of Ms. Winfrey's life, stressing her management abilities and successes
4. Using at least three other references (e.g., books, research-journal articles, newspaper or magazine stories or credible Web sites), post an 800- to 1,000-word Web page that addresses two of the earlier critical thinking questions. Assume that your Web page will be used as an internal reference for a corporation's intranet.
5. Using at least three other references (e.g., books, research-journal articles, newspaper or magazine stories or credible Web sites), write an 800- to 1,000-word essay that addresses two of the earlier critical thinking questions. Assume that your essay will be used as an internal reference for a corporation's business plan.

Taking Risks and Allowing Failures

Roundtable Discussion

BOSSIDY: You've also got to be careful that the only people you retain are those who are risk-averse and don't want to do the dot-com situation. So I say to our people, let's go get some people from the dot-coms right now. They're failing everyday.

(And they're burgeoning everyday. I mean, it's that kind of an industry.)

But at least they showed the interest and the courage to take some risks. And we need those kind of people in the corporation.

COWAN: So in other words, failure can be a good thing? You like failure?

BOSSIDY: I used to hire real estate people. I always hired ones that had failures. Because they all have it.

I wanted the person who had lost a lot of money for somebody else to come work for me. I didn't want to see the ones who were vanilla, who never made a mistake. Because I know they're going to. You're in that business, over time you do.

You don't reward—you don't praise—failure. But it can be a wonderful thing in terms of what you learn.

KOZLOWSKI: But when you have a company the size of Tyco—next year we'll have some $27 billion in sales—there are failures day in and day out in our business. We have people trying products, coming out with new ideas, spending money in marketplaces.

You don't hear about that. You hear about our successes. And fortunately our successes far outweigh our failures. But the important part is that people are trying things. You know, they're having ideas, they're making some assumptions. They're going out into the marketplace.

They have the freedom to do that. And there's no penalty for trying to execute what seemed like a pretty good idea at the time. What we might not have known is, somebody had a better product, or we didn't get to the marketplace fast enough, or —— but you really have to have that type of an environment where people are trying things, you know.

And they may come from a dot-com company and they may be great, but, they may come from some acquisition that we've accomplished.

LYONS: How difficult is it to push that philosophy down into the ranks and have it be believed?

KOZLOWSKI: I think we do it through our incentive programs, through what we talk about. We talk about a few things on a day-in and day-out basis: about decentralization, making your own decisions; we talk about having no penalty for a failure.

We cite examples of people who have come up with ideas, and we tried it, and we backed it, and then learned why it didn't work. I think that with new people coming to the company via our acquisitions, you know there's some skepticism. But, hopefully, over time, that skepticism is overcome.

NEFF: You want to encourage risk-taking. And there's an example in book— the chapter on Jack Welch [of General Electric]—where a team was trying to develop a new lamp. They failed, and he gave them all a TV set for their efforts.

You don't want to discourage people from taking risks.

LAZARUS: But the question's an interesting one because, even from an advertising agency perspective, I can go into a client and, just based on how they react to advertising ideas, I can tell how deep down the comfort with risk-taking is.

So it's obvious, even down at a product-manager level, whether people are being encouraged to take risks or, in fact, whether the first objective is not to make a mistake. Because I can smell that in a minute.

CITRIN: Isn't the issue one of risk/reward? Lou Noto [of Mobil] said in the book, "If you bet $100 with a real chance of winning $500 and you lose, I want to encourage you to find another opportunity like that. Because that's the kind of risk we want to be taking. But if you risk $100 and made $105, I'm going to fire you."

ABELSON: What about when the failure is very public??

KOZLOWSKI: It depends if it's an integrity issue, or if it was a reasonable risk.

If you had reasonable assumptions going in and you were going to try something, then you live with that. But if there was some question on accounting or integrity or not being straightforward, that's different. That needs to be dealt with in a severe way.

BOSSIDY: I think every failure needs to be analyzed. Why? What happened? And sometimes you've got to stand up, yourself, and say, "I was a part of that and that I have as much responsibility for it as anybody does. Now, let's make sure we don't make that same mistake again when we develop another product."

I mean, we're not here to promote failure. But we're here to analyze what things go well and what things aren't, and then try to correct it as you go on. It happens all the time.

But I don't think you want to try to escape it. Because I think it's obvious to your organization if you try to escape it, and that isn't a good message to have communicated.

WANG: I think what you've got to do is take the blame. I mean, ultimately you give all the credit to your people and you take all the blame.

The thing we do at C.A. is, we tell the people we're no smarter than any other company in the world. You know, we have this much time, some finite amount of time, and we make 10 decisions and hopefully get five or six of them right.

The problem with all the other companies seems to be they may spend five times the amount of time to make decisions, spinning about what went wrong: "It's really not my fault." And an avalanche of e-mail, and it goes on and on.

And all of that time could have been used to make decisions. So if we could just cut out all the spinning—and this is what I keep telling my people, just cut that out, as both Larry and Dennis said—if we could cut that out, just that piece of the spinning, then we'll have that much more time. so it's the right to fail, really.

COWAN: So, fire all the P.R. people?

BOSSIDY: No, but I think, to Charles's point: If you go into an organization, Shelly, for example, and make a presentation, and then the first thing they'll say is, "Well, we're going to get a group of people together to study that"—now you know you're in trouble.

I'd rather say, "Shelly, thank you very much, talk to you later."

LAZARUS: I'd rather you did that too.

BOSSIDY: Because I do think, to Charles's point again, I do think that you look at an organization that makes decisions slowly and I'll show you a slow corporation.

You've got to find a way to get at these things sooner and look at the thing as thoroughly as you can, make a decision, and get going.

KOZLOWSKI: Any time you're going to try something, at whatever level, there's always a risk of failure.

BOSSIDY: And if you study it for three months, or study it for a day, probably the percentages are about the same. So you might as well—

WANG: And the solution you proposed three months ago doesn't apply today.

KOZLOWSKI: That's right.

LAZARUS: But I've even had a client say—well, this, to me, was the greatest statement of all—a very senior level client looked at me in a very challenging way and said, "If this is such a great idea, why haven't my competitors done it?" Which I found the most extraordinary question that I thought I had ever been asked.

But what it says is, he did nothing until someone else did it first. And that's a very distinctive kind of organization.

WANG: The answer should have been, "They're not as smart as you."

KOZLOWSKI: They sound like an excellent acquisition candidate.

LAZARUS: They're big. They're really big.

The New York Times, October 10, 1999
http://www.nytimes.com/library/financial/sunday/101099leader-roundtable3-risk.html

CRITICAL THINKING QUESTIONS

1. We have been raised to avoid failure and strive for success. How has such an approach impacted your life?

2. What are the possible negative effects of punishing failure?
3. As a manager, where would you permit failure? At what point would you discipline employees for their failure?

STORY-SPECIFIC QUESTIONS

1. How did Jack Welsh respond to risk-taking?
2. What is the importance of an incentive system when encouraging risk-taking? Explain how it can be used.
3. The discussants contend that there are certain criteria that managers can use to select a risk-taker from a non-risk-taker. What are they?
4. Is it better to bet $100 and make $105, or to bet $100 with a good chance of making $500 and lose? Why?
5. How does risk-taking impact decision-making?

SHORT APPLICATION ASSIGNMENTS

1. In teams or individually, answer the story-specific questions; keep your answers to 25–75 words for each question.
2. In teams of three to five persons, or as a whole class, discuss your responses to the critical thinking questions.
3. Prepare a one-page memo report (200–250 words) to your instructor in which you summarize this article. You will find a model one-page report on the Web site (nytimes.swcollege.com).
4. Write an executive summary (200–250 words). As an administrative assistant to a busy executive, you are expected to summarize selected articles and present important points. You will find a model executive summary on the Web site.
5. Summarize this article (100–125 words) for your company's newsletter. You will find a model newsletter article on the Web site.
6. Individually or in teams, develop an incentive system for rewarding risk taking. Prepare an essay (250–500 words) or a presentation (5–10 minutes) that explains your model.

BUILDING RESEARCH SKILLS

1. Using at least two other articles from the *New York Times* "Roundtable" discussion (www.nytimes.com/library/financial/sunday/101099leader-index.html), compare and contrast them with the current reading. Your instructor may ask you to submit a three- to five-page essay, post a Web page or report your results in a five-minute presentation, along with a letter of transmittal explaining your results.
2. Using at least three other references (e.g., books, research-journal articles, newspaper or magazine stories or credible Web sites), write a 500- to 1,000-word biographical sketch of one of the roundtable participants. What leadership characteristics have made him or her a successful manager?

3. Individually or in teams, develop the criteria that you, as a manager, would use in order to decide when you would punish and reward failure. Your instructor may ask you to submit a three- to five-page essay, post a Web page or report your results in a five-minute presentation, along with a letter of transmittal explaining your results.

4. Using at least three other references (e.g., books, research-journal articles, newspaper or magazine stories or credible Web sites), post an 800- to 1,000-word Web page that addresses two of the earlier critical thinking questions. Assume that your Web page will be used as an internal reference for a corporation's intranet.

5. Using at least three other references (e.g., books, research-journal articles, newspaper or magazine stories or credible Web sites), write an 800- to 1,000-word essay that addresses two of the earlier critical thinking questions. Assume that your essay will be used as an internal reference for a corporation's business plan.

Management and the Role of Attitudes, Values and Ethics

PREVIEW

Over the past several decades, managers have recognized that ethical behavior by management and employees can aid in the growth of a business and make for a productive workplace. Ethical behavior and good business practices can go "hand-in-hand." This chapter explores the interface between organizational ethics, and employee and societal commitments.

The first two articles examine corporate crises brought on, in part, by how managers handled ethical dilemmas. The Hays, Cowell and Whitney story, "How Coke Stumbled in Handling European Contamination Scare," and Barry Meier's "Philip Morris Acknowledges Smoking's Link to Cancer," present similar strategies for crisis management. In both cases, the corporations admitted they were wrong; however, while it took Coca-Cola only months, the tobacco industry took decades to confess.

In addition to ethical communication with consumers, organizations must also consider ethical employee communication. New technologies, especially the Internet, present a host of new employee issues. How should managers cope with the employee problems associated with innovations, such as e-mail? Jeffrey L. Seglin's "You've Got Mail. You're Being Watched" examines how e-mail creates ethical problems in the workplace, and he suggests that new technologies may be the next battleground in employee-management relations.

Source: Christine M. Thompson/CyberTimes

How Coke Stumbled in Handling European Contamination Scare

By Constance L. Hays with Alan Cowell and Craig R. Whitney

As Coca-Cola Co. tries to regain its footing in Europe after a contamination scare that caused the biggest product recall in the company's 113-year history, executives have made a rare admission: that mistakes were made in manufacturing.

Such humility is far from routine for the soft-drink giant, renowned as it is for superb marketing and a corporate structure that is well-oiled from top to bottom. But the crisis in Europe, in which hundreds of people said they felt sick after drinking Cokes, has revealed a different Coca-Cola, one that stumbled repeatedly, making an unfortunate situation even worse.

When the outbreak began, Coke executives took several days to make the matter a high priority. An apology to consumers came more than a week after the first public reports that people had fallen ill. It was not until June 18—10 days after the first schoolboy became dizzy and nauseated after drinking a Coke—that top company officials arrived in Belgium. And when Coke did begin to respond, it attempted to minimize the reports of illness.

"I am genuinely amazed that they have reacted like this, and I don't know what has gone on inside the company to make them react like this," said David Arnold, a Harvard Business School marketing professor who has studied Coke for years.

The cardinal rule of consumer-products marketing is that the customers' perceptions—often divorced from the facts—are what count, he said, adding that a company like Coke, which has built an $18.8 billion business out of sugar water, should know that better than anyone. "They should have said yes, there appears to be a problem, instead of arguing the facts," he said.

It will be weeks before the damage to Coca-Cola can be fully assessed. Analysts have already knocked a few pennies per share off earnings estimates for the current quarter for both Coca-Cola and Coca-Cola Enterprises, Coke's bottler in Belgium. Beyond that, it is clear that in Europe, which accounts for about 26 percent of Coca-Cola's profits, Coke must take aggressive steps to restore its image.

Philippe L'Enfant, a senior executive with Coca-Cola Enterprises, told a Belgian television station on Sunday that the company "perhaps lost control of the situation to a certain extent." While the firm had a crisis management strategy, he said, "The crisis was bigger than any worst-case scenario we could have imagined."

Constance L. Hays with Alan Cowell and Craig R. Whitney

Coca-Cola's muted initial approach to its problems appears to have back-fired. In a news conference in Brussels last week, company chairman M. Douglas Ivester said he had chosen to "take a lower profile on this," at the request of Belgian Health Minister Luc van den Brossche, and other officials of Belgium's government.

Yet Coke had taken a low profile well before any ministers took charge. A bar owner outside Antwerp reported May 12 that four people felt sick after drinking bottles of Coke that smelled strange. That incident did not lead to public safety warnings, although samples were tested, and no mention was made of it after other incidents were reported, beginning June 8, because, a Coca-Cola spokesman said, it was unclear whether they were connected.

Government officials in Belgium and France complained repeatedly about Coca-Cola's apparent inability to tell them, in timely fashion, what it knew. "You can say that since the beginning, Coca-Cola has presented real contradic-tions," said one French official involved in the investigation.

Some of those contradictions were evident within Coke itself. One spokes-man said this week that the May 12 incident was widely known, since it had been "extensively covered in the Belgian press." Another spokesman said min-utes earlier that he had never heard of it.

When the first reports of illness were made June 8, local executives of Coca-Cola Enterprises were called in. That day, a Tuesday, schoolchildren in Bornem who had been sold Coke in 200-centiliter glass bottles by their schools experi-enced dizziness, nausea and other symptoms that ended with 42 of them being hospitalized over the next 24 hours.

Odilon Hermans, the director of the St. Mary school in Bornem, a well-to-do suburb of Brussels, contacted the Coca-Cola Enterprises bottling plant in Antwerp that day. He said several managers visited the school and the hospi-tal before nightfall.

While a Belgian health official said the bottler had recalled several batches of suspect Coke on June 8, it was not until June 10 that remaining unopened bottles at the school were taken away, Hermans said. "It was after we had to push them a little bit in the beginning," he said.

The government decided to get deeply involved on June 10, after eight chil-dren from Bruges, outside Brussels, had to be hospitalized, said Susan Grognard, an assistant to van den Brossche, the Belgian Health Minister. They said they felt sick after drinking cans of Coca-Cola and Fanta, a fruit-flavored brand owned by Coke.

"From that moment, we began following it very closely," said the health of-ficial. Coke executives were summoned to van den Brossche's offices for a meeting the following day.

The meeting took place at noon. About four hours later, the ministry learned that 13 more children had been hospitalized in Harelbeke, showing the same symptoms as the children in Bruges and Bornem.

The news came at a sensitive time. Belgian elections were only two days away. Two ministers had already lost their jobs as a result of an earlier, unrelated scare in which animal feed contaminated with dioxin, a substance that can cause cancer, was found across Belgium.

That evening, the Belgian government informed the European Commission and French officials of the steps it had taken. The Belgians also set up a call center to field questions about Coke. It received more than 200 calls by Monday, June 14. That day, 42 children were taken to the hospital in Lochristi. Eight more were hospitalized in Korttrijk the next day.

As more reports of illness were made, the government ordered Coke to remove its products from schools. The removal was not a perfect process.

"There was a situation where there was a vending machine in a school and the building was locked, and we couldn't get to it over the weekend," said Randy Donaldson, a Coca-Cola spokesman.

On Sunday, voters removed the prime minister from office, and on Monday, the Belgian government ordered all Coke products off the market. Luxembourg enacted its own ban the next day. The government of the Netherlands banned Coke products shipped through Belgium. And health authorities in France asked Coca-Cola to shut down its plant in Dunkirk, near the Belgian border, after Coke said that a substance found on some cans shipped from Dunkirk was not normally used by the company.

Coca-Cola executives said that flawed carbon dioxide, the gas that produces the bubbles in a carbonated soft drink, probably caused the smell some of the Belgian children reported. And the substance on the cans, para-chloro-meta-cresol, was traced to wooden pallets used to transport them from the Dunkirk plant. The pallets, ordered from a Dutch company, used the solvent although it did not meet Coke's specifications, said Robert Pagani, senior vice president for operations at Coca-Cola Enterprises.

As the bans spread in Europe, Coca-Cola resolutely insisted that its products were not bad for anyone. "It may make you feel sick, but it is not harmful," said Rob Baskin, a spokesman at company headquarters in Atlanta.

On June 16, in a statement issued at 10:30 P.M. Brussels time, Ivester issued a terse apology from Atlanta. "We deeply regret any problems experienced by our European consumers," he said.

That day, German officials removed Coke products that had been bottled in France or Belgium. Consumer groups in Germany and elsewhere said the company had been less than direct and was unreassuring in its public explanations, including assertions that the drinks were safe even though people had gotten sick after consuming them.

In responding, Coca-Cola executives displayed a curious indifference to the political and social concerns in Europe, which ranged from fears of dioxin to trade squabbles over bananas, surrounding the events involving their own products. In such an atmosphere, "this would be quite scary to a consumer, because you would assume that Coca-Cola, which is a totally artificial, manufactured product, would not have any problems," Arnold said. "Meat or fruit might be a risk. But not something like Coca-Cola."

Ivester arrived in Brussels for the first time June 18. At one point that day he telephoned James Burke, the chairman of Johnson & Johnson during the Tylenol tampering crisis in the 1980s, and talked "at great length," according to Burke's assistant.

As he did so, regional health authorities in Spain were recalling thousands of cases of Coke products, and Germany warned consumers to be sure their Cokes were made in Germany, to be safe. There were no reports of illness from Germany or Spain, and none from Luxembourg or the Netherlands.

As the bans on Coke products continued into Monday, June 21, Ivester issued a memo to all of his company's 28,000 employees. The subject was the "Belgian Issue," and it said, among other things, that the company's "quality control processes in Belgium faltered." Suggesting there was no cause for alarm, he added: "I have personally tasted the products and held the packages involved with no adverse reaction."

Full-page newspaper advertisements appeared that day in French newspapers, asserting the safety of Coke products and listing a toll-free number for people to call with any safety questions.

At the same time, Coke circulated a toxicologist's report it had commissioned, which concluded that substances found in the products in question—such as hydrogen sulfide and the phenol compound—were present in amounts too small to have caused the symptoms people reported. It fanned rumors, reported in European newspapers, that people who said they got sick were actually experiencing "psychosomatic" illnesses.

Coke ran ads in Belgian newspapers June 22 that consisted of a more contrite apology, topped by a photograph of a smiling Ivester. "I should have spoken to you earlier, and I apologize for that," the ad read. "Over the past several days in Belgium, we allowed two breakdowns to occur in fulfilling the promise of Coca-Cola."

The next day, June 23, Belgium lifted the ban on Coke's bottled and canned soft drinks. Van den Brossche said Coke had agreed to conditions, including more quality control, set by him.

By Friday, all other countries had followed suit, and complaints of illness had, for the moment at least, ceased. An investigation continues in France, focused on the Dunkirk plant. Vending machines remain shut down in Belgium until the authorities check all 11,000 of them.

Tuesday the company announced a recall in Poland, this time of its Bonaqua bottled water. Mold was found growing at the bottom of 1,500 bottles, according to Coke officials, who said it was not dangerous, although Polish health officials said it could cause digestive problems.

The New York Times, June 30, 1999

http://www.nytimes.com/library/financial/063099coke-europe.html

CRITICAL THINKING QUESTIONS

1. Overall, why did Coca-Cola handle this crisis correctly or incorrectly?
2. What general guidelines would you suggest for crisis management?
3. If Coke were given a second chance, how would you suggest that it manage this crisis?
4. What—if any—will be the long-term effects of Coca-Cola's management of this crisis?

STORY-SPECIFIC QUESTIONS

1. What were three mistakes that Coca-Cola made in managing this crisis?
2. How did the Belgian, French and German governments react to this crisis?
3. According to Professor David Arnold of Harvard, what is the cardinal rule of consumer-products marketing?

SHORT APPLICATION ASSIGNMENTS

1. In teams or individually, answer the story-specific questions; keep your answers to 25–75 words for each question.
2. In teams of three to five persons, or as a whole class, discuss your responses to the critical thinking questions.
3. Prepare a one-page memo report (200–250 words) to your instructor in which you summarize this article. You will find a model one-page report on the Web site (nytimes.swcollege.com).
4. Write an executive summary (200–250 words). As an administrative assistant to a busy executive, you are expected to summarize selected articles and present important points. You will find a model executive summary on the Web site.
5. Summarize this article (100–125 words) for your company's newsletter. You will find a model newsletter article on the Web site.
6. In teams of three to five persons, or as a whole class, discuss your school's or organization's crisis management policies. Your instructor may assign you a specific crisis to discuss. You also may be asked to report your results in a five-minute presentation or in a one-page memo.

BUILDING RESEARCH SKILLS

1. Individually or in teams, draft a crisis management policy for a school or organization. Your instructor may give you a sample school or organization. You also may be asked to submit a three- to five-page policy handbook or post a Web page, along with a letter of transmittal explaining the project.
2. Individually or in teams, analyze a school or organization's handling of a crisis. Your instructor may give you a sample crisis. Your instructor may ask you to submit a three- to five-page report, post a Web page or report your results in a five-minute presentation, along with a letter of transmittal explaining your findings.

3. Using at least three other references (e.g., books, research-journal articles, newspaper or magazine stories or credible Web sites), write an 800- to 1,000-word essay that addresses two of the earlier critical thinking questions. Assume that this essay will be used as an internal reference for a school or organization's crisis management plan.
4. Using at least three other references (e.g., books, research-journal articles, newspaper or magazine stories or credible Web sites), post an 800- to 1,000-word Web page that addresses at least two of the earlier critical thinking questions. Assume that this page will be posted in the policy section of a corporate intranet.

Philip Morris Acknowledges Smoking's Link to Cancer

By Barry Meier

Philip Morris is acknowledging that scientific evidence shows that smoking causes lung cancer and other deadly diseases, after decades of disputing the findings of the United States Surgeon General and other medical authorities.

In recent years Philip Morris, the nation's largest cigarette maker, has moved closer to prevailing scientific opinion about the health risks of smoking, as it has faced increasing pressure from smoking-related lawsuits, regulators and Congress.

But on a new Internet site it unveiled on Tuesday as part of a $100 million corporate image campaign, the company unequivocally states there is an "overwhelming medical and scientific consensus that cigarette smoking causes" diseases including lung cancer, emphysema and heart disease.

It also states that smoking "is addictive as that term is most commonly used today."

The move by Philip Morris is part of a trend among tobacco producers to try to put health-related issues behind them after agreeing in the last two years to pay $246 billion to settle lawsuits brought by states seeking to recover their Medicaid costs for treating ill smokers.

By making more disclosures about smoking risks, producers also want to make it harder for those who start smoking now to sue by contending they were unaware of the dangers.

The Brown & Williamson Tobacco Company created a Web site with information on health issues last year, and the R. J. Reynolds Tobacco Company is creating one.

Several anti-smoking advocates who were read the new statements by Philip Morris said they were a marked shift for the company, particularly in the area of smoking and health. Previously, the company had contended, for example, that smoking was a "risk factor" or a "causal factor" in diseases like lung cancer, not that it caused the diseases.

"It is a profound change," said Dr. David A. Kessler, the former head of the Food and Drug Administration who began a Federal effort to regulate tobacco. "It really sets a new stage for regulation and legislation."

Matthew Myers, a lawyer with the Campaign for Tobacco-Free Kids, an advocacy group in Washington, agreed but added that Philip Morris still had not taken the final step.

"The acknowledgments seem to be an abandonment once and for all of the campaign of sowing doubts in the minds of consumers," Myers said. "But it falls a critical step short because it doesn't say whether Philip Morris agrees with these conclusions."

Last year, Geoffrey C. Bible, the company's chairman, testified before a Senate Committee that the company acknowledged that substantial evidence supported the "judgment that smoking plays a causal role" in diseases like lung cancer. Bible also testified that the company recognized that "under some definitions, cigarette smoking is addictive."

Bible declined on Tuesday to be interviewed. But responding to Myers's comments, Steven Parrish, a senior vice president at Philip Morris, said Philip Morris was "not going to dispute that smoking causes cancer."

He added, however, that the company still would require any plaintiff in a lawsuit to prove that their disease was caused by smoking rather than any other factor.

Parrish added that the change in Philip Morris's position was not the result of any new scientific findings. He said it had come because the company had decided to take a less combative and defensive position.

Asked why Philip Morris had not changed its stance earlier, he said, "That is all water under the bridge."

The company's new Internet site (www.philipmorris.com) is one part of the Philip Morris campaign intended to reshape its corporate image. Company officials said they would spend $100 million annually on the effort, which will include television advertisements emphasizing the company's charitable activities.

As part of the campaign, Philip Morris will also play down its role as a cigarette maker. For example, while the company Web site will contain the logos of two of its major divisions, Kraft Foods and Miller Brewing, it does not show the distinctive logo of the Philip Morris tobacco division or the red-and-white chevron of its leading brand, Marlboro.

Parrish also said another goal of the campaign would be to redirect the often-acrimonious debate about smoking into a constructive one.

"This is a serious and good faith effort on our part to try to engage in a dialogue," he said.

Last year, Brown & Williamson Tobacco, a division of B.A.T. Industries P.L.C., revised its Internet site to reflect its stance on smoking and health issues. On it the company states it "believes that it is appropriate for the public health community to conclude and warn the public that cigarette smoking causes certain diseases."

Tommy Payne, an official of R. J. Reynolds, said the company was also creating a Web site. Payne said he believed the industry effort followed a recently settled round of lawsuits between cigarette makers and state attorneys general.

In those lawsuits, the states argued that cigarette makers should reimburse them for the cost of smoking-related health care costs because they had misled the public by vigorously disputing Government findings about smoking and disease.

"This is a new phase from a manufacturer's standpoint of how you talk about the issues surrounding cigarettes," Payne said.

As part of an earlier agreement between tobacco companies and state officials that collapsed in Congress last year, cigarette companies would have agreed not to have disputed public health findings about links between smoking and disease.

Tobacco producers, however, still face numerous legal problems. Last month, the Federal Government filed a major lawsuit that charges cigarette makers with fraud and seeks to recover billions in health care expenses.

Still, Dr. Kessler, the former F.D.A. Administrator, said he believed that the recent steps by Philip Morris were important in that they might give cigarette makers an opportunity to act on decisions they might have made decades ago.

"The tobacco industry could have gone down this road in 1964 but decided instead to engage in a campaign of fraud and deception that it is now paying for," he said.

The New York Times, October 13, 1999
http://www.nytimes.com/library/politics/101399tobacco-warning.html

CRITICAL THINKING QUESTIONS

1. In public relations, the dictum is "honesty is the best policy." When considering a response to an organizational crisis, how honest should a manager be? What should a manager say and not say?
2. Compare and contrast the Philip Morris strategy with the Coca-Cola approach to dealing with a public relations crisis.
3. Management critics castigate business for unethical practices. They insist that good business practices and ethical behavior go "hand-in-hand." Explain why.
4. What is the relationship between ethics and business success? Is there one? If so, defend your viewpoint. If not, what arguments might you offer against the relationship between ethics and profitable business practices?

STORY-SPECIFIC QUESTIONS

1. Philip Morris' admission was related to what two factors?
2. Matthew Myers, a lawyer for the Campaign for Tobacco-Free Kids, approved of the Philip Morris statement but argues that the company had "not taken the final step." In Myers' opinion, what is the final step?
3. How will Philip Morris play down its role as a cigarette maker?
4. In spite of the tobacco companies admission of the link between smoking and cancer, they still face serious legal problems. What are they?

SHORT APPLICATION ASSIGNMENTS

1. In teams or individually, answer the story-specific questions; keep your answers to 25–75 words for each question.

2. In teams of three to five persons, or as a whole class, discuss your responses to the critical thinking questions.

3. Prepare a one-page memo report (200–250 words) to your instructor in which you summarize this article. You will find a model one-page report on the Web site (nytimes.swcollege.com).

4. Write an executive summary (200–250 words). As an administrative assistant to a busy executive, you are expected to summarize selected articles and present important points. You will find a model executive summary on the Web site.

5. Summarize this article (100–125 words) for your company's newsletter. You will find a model newsletter article on the Web site.

6. If you were the manager in charge of public relations for Philip Morris, how would you have responded to the crisis? Develop crisis management plan (250–500 words) for Philip Morris.

BUILDING RESEARCH SKILLS

1. Using at least three references (e.g., books, research-journal articles, newspaper or magazine stories or credible Web sites), be prepared to debate, pro or con, Philip Morris' strategy to admit the link between smoking and cancer. Was the decision wise? Or was the decision a strategic error? Your instructor may assign you a side to take.

2. Research how one other organization (e.g., the U.S. Postal Service) has dealt with public relations crisis. Cite at least two references. Your instructor may ask you to submit a three- to five-page report, post a Web page or report your results in a five-minute presentation, along with a letter of transmittal explaining your findings.

3. Visit the Philip Morris Internet site (www.philipmorris.com) and review the company's statement on smoking and health. Does the company say why it is now admitting the link between smoking and health risks? Does the company offer a reason for its admission? Did it admit any responsibility for the long term "cover-up" of the dangers of smoking? Your instructor may ask you to submit a three- to five-page report, post a Web page or report your results in a five-minute presentation, along with a letter of transmittal explaining your findings.

4. Using at least three other references (e.g., books, research-journal articles, newspaper or magazine stories or credible Web sites), write an 800- to 1,000-word essay that addresses two of the earlier critical thinking questions. Assume that this essay will be used as an internal reference for a school or an organization's crisis management plan.

5. Using at least three other references (e.g., books, research-journal articles, newspaper or magazine stories or credible Web sites), post an 800- to 1,000-word Web page that addresses at least two of the earlier critical thinking questions. Assume that this page will be posted in the policy section of a corporate intranet.

You've Got Mail. You're Being Watched.

By Jeffrey L. Seglin

"It was tragic," recalled Mary Beth Heying, a principal at Edward Jones & Company, the brokerage firm in St. Louis. In April, an employee had complained to the human resources department after receiving an e-mail containing inappropriate material, meaning off-color jokes, pornography and so on. "We investigated and found that a large number of associates were involved" in distributing such messages, Ms. Heying said. Depending on "the egregiousness of their involvement," she said, the company dismissed 19, warned 41 and allowed 1 to resign.

The company has a "very clear" written policy on e-mail, Ms. Heying said. Some 2,700 of its 17,000 employees have e-mail or Internet access at work (none of the brokers do, because written communication is heavily regulated in the brokerage industry), and each of the 2,700 was given a copy of the policy when receiving e-mail access, Ms. Heying said.

An American Management Association survey this year found that 27 percent of companies do what Edward Jones does—monitor internal e-mail—up from 20.2 percent in 1998. In the vast majority of cases, employees are informed of the surveillance.

There is little dispute that companies have both the power and the legal right to monitor e-mail sent on the company network on company time. But there are conflicting ethical imperatives at work when managers consider a monitoring policy: on the one hand, to avoid unwarranted intrusions into employees' privacy; on the other, to keep unchecked circulation of off-color jokes and other inappropriate material from creating a hostile atmosphere.

Allan A. Kennedy, a management consultant and co-author of *The New Corporate Cultures* (Perseus, 1999), starts from the premise that "companies that monitor e-mail traffic or use the power of modern technology to act as Big Brother to the employees are dehumanizing the work environment." Still, he sees a need for policing e-mail, given how it can expose a company to litigation. He says the best approach is to let workers frame the policy.

"An employee-based e-mail monitoring system would not be as disrespectful," he said. "It would be from one employee to another, saying 'We don't want to work in an environment where this kind of thing goes on.' It'd be equivalent to the kind of natural monitoring that would have gone on around the water cooler."

In reality, though, monitoring is rarely continuous; far more often it is used only when a company has someone or something to investigate—when, as at Edward Jones, an employee complains about a particular message. Indeed, Laura P. Hartman, a professor of business ethics at the University of Wisconsin,

You've Got Mail. You're Being Watched. **93**

Jeffrey L. Seglin

thinks the *threat* of monitoring may be seen as a strong-enough deterrent that companies can spare themselves from much actual monitoring.

Employers are naturally uneasy about unmasking inappropriate e-mail and dismissing offenders.

But invasion of privacy isn't the root of the unease; the distress of firing is. Most managers dread having to do something so painful to the person across the desk. "We have a zero tolerance policy with regard to inappropriate e-mail, and people know that," Ms. Heying said. "Does that mean we didn't feel badly about 20 associates? Oh, by all means, we do."

E-mail takes companies into new ethical territory, as they struggle with controlling a technology so utterly different from other communications tools. Unlike a phone call or hallway conversation, e-mail leaves an audit trail that can pinpoint the abuser. But unlike a paper memo, e-mail moves at lightning speed, both in delivery and in composition, often with little reflection or second thought. It will probably be awhile before there is corporate consensus on the fairest balance between privacy and protection.

Until then, the responsibility to do the right thing falls upon employees, who can use common sense as a guide.

If an employee's passion for e-mail privacy is born of a desire not to have the boss find out he's been placing bids all day for vintage comic books in an on-line auction, chances are he already knows he shouldn't be doing that at work.

In this new high-technology world, a remarkably old-fashioned rule of thumb applies: Don't do what you wouldn't want to be caught doing.

The New York Times, July 18, 1999
http://www.nytimes.com/library/tech/99/07/biztech/articles/18ethics.html

CRITICAL THINKING QUESTIONS

1. What are the pros and cons of e-mail policies that restrict employee use of e-mail to business only? What are the benefits and costs to managers? What are the benefits and costs to employees?
2. As a manager, would you restrict the use of e-mail to business only? Would you make exceptions? If so, for what and under what circumstances?
3. Organizations contend that they have the right to monitor employee e-mail. The author suggests that there is an another viewpoint. What is it? What is your opinion?

STORY-SPECIFIC QUESTIONS

1. Do companies have a legal right to monitor e-mail?
2. The article contends that e-mail transports companies into a "new ethical territory." Explain the comment.
3. What is the old-fashioned rule of thumb mentioned in the article?
4. What is the financial cost to the company of monitoring e-mail systems?

SHORT APPLICATION ASSIGNMENTS

1. In teams or individually, answer the story-specific questions; keep your answers to 25–75 words for each question.
2. In teams of three to five persons, or as a whole class, discuss your responses to the critical thinking questions.
3. Prepare a one-page memo report (200–250 words) to your instructor in which you summarize this article. You will find a model one-page report on the Web site nytimes.swcollege.com).
4. Write an executive summary (200–250 words). As an administrative assistant to a busy executive, you are expected to summarize selected articles and present important points. You will find a model executive summary on the Web site.
5. Summarize this article (100–125 words) for your company's newsletter. You will find a model newsletter article on the Web site.
6. Assume you manage a small software company with 100 employees. As a manager, formulate an e-mail policy for your employees, and justify it. Individually or in teams prepare a class presentation or write an essay (250–500 words) outlining your policy and the supporting rationale.

BUILDING RESEARCH SKILLS

1. Research the American Civil Liberties Union Web site (www.aclu.org/) concerning its views on electronic monitoring. Summarize at least three reports or press releases. Your instructor may ask you to submit a three- to five-page report, post a Web page or report your results in a five-minute presentation, along with a letter of transmittal explaining your findings.
2. Individually or in teams, draft an e-mail monitoring policy for your school or organization. Your instructor may ask you to submit a three- to five-page report, post a Web page or report your results in a five-minute presentation, along with a letter of transmittal explaining your findings.
3. Using at least three other references (e.g., books, research-journal articles, newspaper or magazine stories or credible Web sites), write an 800- to 1,000-word essay that addresses two of the earlier critical thinking questions. Assume that this essay will be used as an internal reference for a school or an organization's crisis management plan.
4. Using at least three other references (e.g., books, research-journal articles, newspaper or magazine stories or credible Web sites), post an 800- to 1,000-word Web page that addresses at least two of the earlier critical thinking questions. Assume that this page will be posted in the policy section of a corporate intranet.

Management and the Future

PREVIEW

This closing chapter captures trends that may influence tomorrow's workplace. They are not necessarily major trends; rather, they are "snap-shots" of how things may be.

In "It's Long Boom or Bust For Leading Futurist," Steve Lohr examines the ideas of futurist Peter Schwartz, who predicts the "Long Boom," an unprecedented global economic expansion fueled by the free market and technological change.

To survive in boom or bust, managers must learn from other segments of the economy, as Corey Kilgannon explains in "What Sex Sites Can Teach Everyone Else." And believe it or not, pornography is one role model for online businesses looking to profit from today's economic and technological changes. Cyber-skin entrepreneurs were one of the first merchants to make e-commerce pay—and theirs is still one of the most profitable Internet sectors.

Finally, David Leonhardt explores a unique style of management: no manager whatsoever. As "A Leaderless Orchestra Offers Lessons for Business" illustrates, the ultimate flat organization has no hierarchical

An Orpheus rehearsal at Baruch College gives business students a chance to gain some lessons on leadership.

Source: Jack Manning/The New York Times

structure at all. It must work, though; the Orpheus orchestra won three Grammy awards in 1999 and is a permanent fixture at Carnegie Hall. Hundreds of American companies are also flattening by trimming the management layers between top executives and people in the field.

It's Long Boom or Bust for Leading Futurist

By Steve Lohr

SAN FRANCISCO—Peter Schwartz is a professional marketer of big, brow-furrowing ideas. By 2020, he says, the internal combustion engine will probably have gone the way of the dodo bird as conventional automobiles are replaced by hybrid cars powered by fuel cells that mostly use hydrogen.

A telecommunications revolution, Schwartz believes, is coming even sooner. Thanks to big satellite projects, connections for high-speed Internet, telephone and video will be commonplace in six years or so. The world will be wired, inexpensively. By 2005, teenagers in villages in developing countries will be chatting on videophones as they surf the Net.

By 2010, Schwartz predicts, breakthroughs in biotechnology and gene therapy may enable science to reverse aging and extend life. The prospect here, he insists, is not merely a prolonged old age but living for decades in one's biological '40s.

Yet these are mere ingredients of Schwartz's biggest idea, which he calls the "Long Boom." Its thesis is that the world is witnessing what Schwartz calls "the beginnings of a global economic boom on a scale never experienced before," driven by waves of fundamental technological change and free-market economics.

The Long Boom, which he sees running through about 2020, is a vision of almost unabashed technological optimism about the future from Schwartz, a leading futurist and chairman of the Global Business Network, a research and consulting firm. His manifesto first appeared as a cover story last summer in *Wired* magazine, whose pages generally celebrate the virtues of technology.

Ever since, he has found himself at the center of a spirited debate about technology and the future. Bearded, affable and articulate, Schwartz is a skillful salesman who has won supporters for his ambitious idea, but he has been roundly criticized as well.

In March, a loose-knit group calling itself the "Technorealism Project" emerged. Among the tenets proclaimed on its Web site at www.technorealism. org is the assertion, "The Internet is revolutionary, not utopian."

Andrew Shapiro, a fellow at the Harvard Law School's Center for the Internet and Society and a founder of the Technorealism Project, said, "We're just skeptical of the kind of sheer boosterism that Peter Schwartz is promoting."

Schwartz recently debated the merits of the Long Boom with Daniel Yankelovich, the public opinion analyst and president of Public Agenda, a research organization, at a conference in San Diego. In Yankelovich's view, the Long Boom betrays a "remarkable naïvete" not only about technology but also about the working of market economics. "The market is great at distributing economic goodies," Yankelovich said, "but it doesn't have all these moral virtues that Peter Schwartz attributes to it."

Such reactions, Schwartz says, are precisely why he wrote the Long Boom. It has provoked thought and, he insists, changed the debate about the future. The Long Boom, he asserts, represents "a better vision of what could be if we make the right choices; it is what I think could and should happen."

As a futurist, Schwartz has impressive credentials. An alumnus of the Stanford Research Institute, now SRI International, he led a planning team at the Royal Dutch/Shell Group in London from 1982 to 1986. One of three possibilities drawn up in 1982 by Schwartz and his team was that oil prices would collapse.

That possibility was taken seriously by Shell's senior management, which piled up cash to prepare. After prices fell precipitously, Shell began a $3.5 billion buying spree in 1986, buying oilfields and locking in a long-term cost advantage over most of its rivals.

The Shell legacy gave Schwartz and four colleagues a head start in attracting corporate clients when they founded the Global Business Network in 1988. "Everybody wanted the Shell magic," he recalled.

The Global Business Network, known as GBN, is no ordinary consulting firm. Based in Emeryville, California, where it occupies a converted factory in the shadow of the Bay Bridge, GBN is eclectic if not eccentric. Its character is evident in the backgrounds of its five founders. Besides Schwartz, they are Jay Ogilvy, a former philosophy teacher at Yale University who headed values and lifestyles research at SRI International; Napier Collyns, who spent 30 years in Shell's planning group; Stewart Brand, creator of the *Whole Earth Catalog* and a founder of the Well computer network, and Lawrence Wilkinson, former president of Colossal Pictures.

Today, GBN is a small but thriving specialist firm. Compared with mainstream consultants like McKinsey & Co. or Andersen Consulting, GBN is minuscule. Its revenues are running at $10 million a year, about double the level in 1994, while its staff has also doubled, to 55 people. (McKinsey says it has 4,500 consultants in 81 countries.)

GBN has roughly 100 clients, about half of which sent executives to the company's four-day annual conference in San Francisco last month. The client list is as eclectic as the firm, ranging from IBM and AT&T to the Pentagon, the government of Singapore and the National Education Association.

The conference concluded with an advance screening of the Dreamworks SKG movie "Deep Impact," which has since become a box-office hit. GBN worked with Dreamworks on developing the film, and Schwartz and a few other GBN members are mentioned in the film's credits.

The narrative spine of "Deep Impact" is how people behave in the months after they learn that a comet is going to collide with Earth. The movie, in essence, illustrates the fulcrum of scenario building—a what-if question. And creating scenarios is GBN's specialty.

At the San Francisco conference, four scenarios for the next decade were presented as narratives for the participants to read and debate. They ranged from crisis and decline to an equivalent of the Long Boom, all rendered in imaginative detail.

In the gloom-and-doom scenario, for example, the year 2000 computer bug and global warming are culprits in the tailspin. The European Union is shattered, the Middle East has water shortages, oil prices surge and inflation is ignited. In 2003, the scenario said, "the Dow plummeted from 10,000 to 6,000 in a matter of months." In Mexico, the economy crumbles, South American drug cartels move in, guerrilla wars flare and refugees flood north. "In 2010," the scenario asserted, "President Wilson sent in the U.S. Army to establish order in Mexico."

Certainly provocative and undoubtedly more entertaining than most business reading, but what use is this kind of thing to corporations? Most companies say the GBN scenarios—whether broad ones, like those presented at the San Francisco conference, or ones tailored for specific industries or nations—are useful mainly as complementary planning tools.

The scenarios are built upon in-depth research of demographic, political and technology trends. Daniel McGrath, a business strategy consultant at IBM, said the scenarios then sketched out "causative chains that stretch your imagination and broaden your thinking."

GBN tries to broaden its own thinking through a network of about 100 people in diverse fields. They include Francis Fukuyama, the political scientist; Bruce Sterling, a science fiction writer, and Donella Meadows, an environmentalist. Yet the membership roster is heavy with technophiles including Danny Hillis, a computer scientist and research fellow at Walt Disney; Esther Dyson, an author and newsletter publisher, and John Gage, chief scientist at Sun Microsystems.

Another GBN member is Kevin Kelly, the executive editor of *Wired*. Both GBN and Schwartz personally were original investors in *Wired*, a fact not mentioned in the magazine when it published Schwartz's Long Boom article. "It's very incestuous in some ways," Schwartz allowed.

For $35,000 a year, corporate clients get to join the GBN network members on the company's private web site to discuss all sorts of subjects, from the future of the car to computing's millennium bug.

In addition, clients are mailed two books a month, selected by Schwartz and Brand. "We've basically solved the problem of executives' reading guilt," Schwartz observed. Recent selections include *Remaking Eden*, about cloning by Lee M. Silver, and *The Commanding Heights*, a history of the triumph of free-market policies, by Daniel Yergin and Joseph Stanislaw.

GBN has prospered in recent years, partly because so many corporations,

Some Visions
Peter Schwartz foresees a "long boom" of growth driven by technology. Here are some of its ingredients:
- By 2005, phone and high-speed Internet access for everyone.
- By 2010, gene therapies to reverse aging.
- By 2015, simultaneous language translation, made possible by computer chips 100 times more powerful than today's.
- By 2020, the death of the internal combustion engine. Cars are powered by hydrogen fuel cells.

Some Stumbles
Though often prescient, Peter Schwartz has also misread the future:
- In 1981, he was an author of a book that assumed oil prices were on their way to $85 a barrel.
- In the early 1980s, he was too gloomy about the prospects for the American economy. He failed to understand the entrepreneurial impact of the PC industry.
- In 1994, he missed the Mexican financial crisis. He was the host of a conference on Mexico's future a few weeks before, but did not consider the possibility.

observing developments like the end of the Cold War to the rise of the Internet, sense that change is accelerating. Divining traits of an uncertain future, more than ever, seems an essential corporate survival skill.

But GBN has also done a deft job of marketing its mainstay business of scenario building. "Scenarios have become the leading tool in thinking about the future, and GBN is the best at it," noted Michael Marien, editor of the *Future Survey*, a monthly newsletter.

A central tenet of the discipline, Schwartz wrote in his 1991 book, *The Art of the Long View*, is that "scenarios are not predictions.

"It is simply not possible to predict the future with certainty," he wrote. "Rather, scenarios are vehicles for helping people learn." Scenarios are typically presented in groups of three or four, not alone.

Yet the Long Boom concept appears to be more a prediction than a scenario. And Schwartz, planning experts say, is taking a real risk with his reputation by championing the Long Boom. Professionals in the field of forecasting will talk cautiously about reducing uncertainty, while predictions suggest the huckster-ish world of crystal balls, soothsayers and shamans.

"I think you are moving down a dangerous slope in this business if you become identified with one view of the future," said Paul Saffo, a director for the Institute of the Future, a research organization.

Schwartz acknowledges that risk, but he feels it is worth taking. "I wanted to influence the future," he said.

And Schwartz is an inherent optimist—a trait reinforced by his personal life and his professional experience. His parents were survivors of Nazi concentration camps. Schwartz was born in a refugee camp in 1946, outside Stuttgart, Germany, and lived until he was 5 in a Norwegian refugee camp. His family then immigrated to New Jersey, living in one room of a brownstone.

His father, Benjamin, a self-trained engineer, quickly became a model of post war upward mobility, steadily increasing his skills and income. He ended up designing advanced computer systems, and the family moved to a wealthy suburb of Philadelphia.

Professionally, Schwartz said, he has missed trends most often because of a failure to grasp the forces behind positive outcomes. In the early 1980s, he said, he consistently misread the outlook for the American economy because he failed to imagine the entrepreneurial effect of new industries led by the personal computer business.

"It was a big miss, and that was a real learning experience for me," he said.

The New York Times, June 1, 1998
http://www.nytimes.com/library/tech/98/06/biztech/articles/01futurist.html

CRITICAL THINKING QUESTIONS

1. Futurists have predicted gloom and doom. They have also predicted prosperity. In your estimation, what does the future portend over the next 20 years and why?
2. Based on your answer to question 1, what special challenges will tomorrow's managers encounter?
3. We are now in the midst of a technological revolution. Will societal groups allow this to continue? Or, will segments of the public rebel against rapid technological change? What segments might rebel and why?
4. In Chapter 3, advocates of chaos and complexity warned against planning in today's economy. Nevertheless, we are willing to consider the ideas of Peter Schwartz, who is planning 20 plus years into the future. How would you compare and contrast Schwartz's view with those who espouse complexity and chaos?

STORY-SPECIFIC QUESTIONS

1. What separates GBM from the standard consulting firm?
2. Rather than trying to predict the future, GBM relies on "scenarios." Explain why?
3. Although Schwartz contends that we cannot predict the future, he nevertheless subscribes to the Long Boom theory. Why?

SHORT APPLICATION ASSIGNMENTS

1. In teams or individually, answer the story-specific questions; keep your answers to 25–75 words for each question.
2. In teams of three to five persons, or as a whole class, discuss your responses to the critical thinking questions.
3. Prepare a one-page memo report (200–250 words) to your instructor in which you summarize this article. You will find a model one-page report on the Web site (nytimes.swcollege.com).
4. Write an executive summary (200–250 words). As an administrative assistant to a busy executive, you are expected to summarize selected articles and present important points. You will find a model executive summary on the Web site.
5. Summarize this article (100–125 words) for your company's newsletter. You will find a model newsletter article on the Web site.

BUILDING RESEARCH SKILLS

1. Research the Technological Realism Project Web site. What is it? What ideas do its members subscribe to and promote? Your instructor may ask you to submit a three- to five-page essay, post a Web page or report your results in a five-minute presentation, along with a letter of transmittal explaining your results.
2. In dyads or in groups, use at least three other references (e.g., books, research-journal articles, newspaper or magazine stories or credible Web sites), to prepare a debate, pro or con, on Schwartz's view of the Long Boom.

What Sex Sites Can Teach Everyone Else

By Corey Kilgannon

Where can an e-business struggling to fend off rising competition turn for a model of how to make money on the Web? To the entrepreneurs who were the first to make e-commerce pay and whose businesses are still the most profitable sector of the Internet: the online pornographers.

Not only does the cyberskin game hold lessons for all sorts of online businesses, experts say, but pornography sites have pioneered technical and marketing developments that are at the heart of the business plans of many enterprises that would not be caught dead on the same server.

"There are a lot of lessons to be had from the online porn's success on the Web," said David Zinman, the vice president for marketing of Adknowledge of Palo Alto, California, which charges site owners to gauge how well their online advertisements generate leads and sales.

Mark Tiarra, whose online company, the Tiarra Corporation, creates advertisements and strategies for sex-oriented Web sites, said that compared with his clients and their competitors, "the nonadult side of the Web has always been a year behind the curve in marketing strategies."

This innovative streak has been shaped by two realities: unlike many other Web businesses, sex sites have a product that people are willing to pay for but that almost anyone can produce.

There would be no sex sites if sex did not sell.

"Unlike major mainstream companies, sex sites had no off-line revenue stream," said Tiarra, who is also president of United Adult Sites, a trade organization of 500 online sex companies. "You have to make it on your own."

Early on, visiting sex sites meant long downloads and slow video clips, but operators found ways to send large pictures despite narrow bandwidths.

As the Internet became awash with sex sites, the operators scrambled to develop a way to use existing online technology to get pictures to Web surfers for the few moments they would land on a site.

With income essentially based on speed of content flow, Web site designers began writing programs that tweaked technology to make pages and photos load more quickly to grab their share of the market.

The resulting sites were not always coherent and flowing, but they delivered the product quickly, and that drew browsers and kept them from skipping to the next sex site.

Creators of sex sites used tips and tricks in writing Web page scripts so that sexy selling points loaded onto the screen first before less appetizing elements, like sign-up fees.

Most of the Web's sex sites make money by charging for entry to a video gallery, usually by a membership bought with a credit card. Many also carry paid advertisements for larger sites. Free sites profit by carrying links to other sites, which pay fractions of a cent each time a customer clicks through.

With profits tied to traffic on the site, the battle for the most clicks was on. Some site operators designed tricks to lure casual surfers to accidentally visit sex sites. Some devised loops to repeatedly click onto sites, including manipulation of the back key to keep reloading a page.

Stealth redirection techniques cropped up, including writing programs to create pop-up browsers that emerged as users left sites, creating a "no exit" barrage of windows and prompts. Web sites began feeding encoded key words for sites unrelated to sex into search engines, drawing unsuspecting browsers and causing pop-up advertisements to appear when certain key words were entered.

They bought rights to commonly used names of web sites with altered suffixes. For example, browsers seeking the Presidential web site at www. Whitehouse.gov/ got a sex site if they type in www.Whitehouse.com by mistake.

Some sites began requesting credit card information as proof of age for "free trials," adding in fine print that membership charges automatically would begin afterward.

Early on, Tiarra said, mainstream web site owners were more complacent. "They were coming into this saying, 'Is this going to work?'" he said. "We came in saying, 'How am I going to make enough money to quit my job.'"

Now, he said, mainstream companies are hiring designers of sex sites. "They're looking for successful strategies, so they're going to get the guys who had the most competitors," he said.

Jane Duvall, who assesses sex-oriented sites, said there was a limit to what mainstream sites could copy from the pornographic ones. "The problem with copying porn sites is that sex is the compelling content, and you can never really compete with that," Ms. Duvall said.

But for all the field's ferocious rivalry, sex sites offer lessons in the benefits of cooperation, too, said Ms. Duvall, a former newspaper advertising saleswoman who two years ago used $500 and an old Power Mac to set up her own Web site, Jane's Net Sex Guide, which reviews and rates sites. "We call it co-opetition, and you don't see it much on the nonadult sites," she said. "Even a link trade is a big deal. You're only sending away a user that is leaving anyway."

Mainstream companies using click-through referrals should research the sex-site industry to learn how to avoid getting cheated, she said.

The smaller online pornography sites formed larger networks offering comprehensive memberships and then splitting the profits—resembling America Online's more recent decision to develop an electronic network that would allow members to shop at many retail web sites with one credit account.

They also formed large, free supersites, where each company would post its own click-through banner.

Another example of the strategy of cross-linking or link-swapping was the formation of referral rings, networks in which sites refer customers to one another. Sophisticated tracking systems were then designed to count the referrals that became paying customers, so sites could reward one another with a percentage of the sign-up fee. This practice has been adopted by many mainstream sites, like Amazon.com and Beyond.com.

"The online porn industry has driven Web technology just as it has with all new media," said Seth Warshavsky, the chief executive of the Internet Entertainment Group, a sex-oriented online company based in Seattle.

"The adult industry entrepreneurs have been a lot more aggressive developing marketing strategies because they see a direct return on everything they put out," he said. "They're all players willing to take a risk to develop new marketing strategies, and only now are a lot of the mainstream online companies applying those concepts. We began working video into Web browsers in 1995. Now it's being used all over the Web."

Caity McPherson, the president of Bay Area Adult Sites, a coalition of 100 people who work in the sex-oriented Web site industry, created the sex site, Juicymango.com in 1997. Now she auditions strippers for Rouze.com, a Web site to be introduced on September 9 that offers editorial material on subjects aimed at affluent men, like martinis, cigars and etiquette. It also offers erotic content, but its editors will not use traditional Internet pornography marketing strategies, Ms. McPherson said.

"I suggested we use some synergy links to create partnerships with other sites and increase traffic," she said. "But the editors said, 'Why would we want to get rid of our traffic?'

"They don't understand the sex sites are like a loop that generates more traffic, and the mainstream sites are like a rope where you just fall off when you exit.

Playing by the mainstream rules means keeping your Web site an enclosed little world.

"I live in Silicon Valley," she said, "and when I tell people at meetings I'm from the adult industry, everyone sort of gets all uptight, but afterward a few always give me a card and say, 'Please call me to talk about marketing strategies.'"

Many experts agree that most mainstream sites will never be able to match the pure profit potential of sex sites, which have little overhead and an eager audience.

"One thing that pornography has been more successful at is tapping into two revenue streams, advertising and selling subscriptions," Zinman said. "Only sites offering incredibly high-demand content can get both. Most nonadult sites have advertising, but few can sell subscriptions because you can get the content somewhere else."

Keeping it Out of Your House

After the United States Supreme Court overturned a 1997 Federal law that prohibited the dissemination of sexually explicit material over the Internet in a manner available to children, the market became flooded with software filters for blocking pornography from personal computers.

Most Internet service providers and some Web browsers also offer optional built-in filter services for customers who want to censor Internet material.

Here are some of the filters endorsed by the Federal Communications Commission:

AMERICA ONLINE (www.aol.com) offers as part of its membership fee optional parental controls that block E-mail messages from specific senders and confine access to certain sites. (800) 827-6364

CYBERSITTER (www.cybersitter.com) blocks sites the customer chooses and those from a list compiled and updated regularly by the company. $39.95 (800) 388-2761

CYBER PATROL (www.cyberpatrol.com) selects objectionable sites and updates the list daily; software also filters sites with objectionable words or images. $29.95 (800) 828-2608

CYBERSNOOP (www.pearlsw.com) monitors sites visited. $49.95 (800) 732-7596

NET NANNY (www.netnanny.com) masks offensive words or shuts down browser that accesses banned sites. $39.95 (800) 340-7177

SURFWATCH (www.surfwatch.com) lists 25,000 banned sites. $49.95 (800) 458-6600

He added: "In the porn industry, you have a tremendous demand for the material product. Nonadult industry has to acquire the kind of information that consumers will want to pay for to make a profitable business model. Until then, profitable mainstream web sites will continue to be an oxymoron."

The New York Times, September 9, 1999

http://www.nytimes.com/library/tech/99/09/biztech/technology/22kilg.html

CRITICAL THINKING QUESTIONS

1. What can other managers and entrepreneurs learn from the pornography industry?

2. Why might the business practices of the pornography industry fail in more traditional retail, on-line businesses?
3. If you were starting an on-line marketing business for retail products such as clothes, what specific pornography industry practices might you emulate?

STORY-SPECIFIC QUESTIONS

1. One of the innovations that on-line pornography marketers developed was speed. What was the importance of speed for marketing?
2. How do free sites profit in the pornography industry?
3. Stealth redirection programs are also a favorite tool of pornography sites. Give an example of one.
4. Jane Duval, a sex-site critic, believes that mainstream marketers can only learn so much from sex sites on the Web. Why does Zinman agree?
5. How have sex sites pioneered a spirit of cooperation?

SHORT APPLICATION ASSIGNMENTS

1. In teams or individually, answer the story-specific questions; keep your answers to 25–75 words for each question.
2. In teams of three to five persons, or as a whole class, discuss your responses to the critical thinking questions.
3. Prepare a one-page memo report (200–250 words) to your instructor in which you summarize this article. You will find a model one-page report on the Web site (ny-times.swcollege.com).
4. Write an executive summary (200–250 words). As an administrative assistant to a busy executive, you are expected to summarize selected articles and present important points. You will find a model executive summary on the Web site.
5. Summarize this article (100–125 words) for your company's newsletter. You will find a model newsletter article on the Web site.
6. The article suggests that pornography marketing strategies may not apply to main-line organizations. Write an essay (250–500 words) or prepare a presentation (10 minutes) explaining why. Use arguments listed in the article, together with your own rationale.

BUILDING RESEARCH SKILLS

1. In teams or individually, visit two Web sites of companies offering filtering software. Your instructor may ask you to submit a three- to five-page essay, post a Web page or report your results in a five-minute presentation, along with a letter of transmittal explaining your results.
2. The article includes links to related *New York Times* stories. Review at least two stories. Your instructor may ask you to submit a three- to five-page summary, post a Web page or report your results in a five-minute presentation, along with a letter of transmittal explaining your results.

A Leaderless Orchestra Offers Lessons for Business

By David Leonhardt

NEW YORK—It seemed to be magic. Music burst forth from two dozen string and wind instruments in perfect synchronization, without a conductor to summon it.

An hour later, during a break, the business school students who had been watching the chamber orchestra rehearse had the same question: How did you all start playing at the same moment? "Body gestures," Eriko Sato, the first violinist on the piece, Telemann's "Water Music," said as she shrugged her shoulders to demonstrate. The musicians watch one another closely, they explained, and as each new movement begins, they know where to look for their cue.

This is Orpheus, the orchestra with no conductor and the ultimate flat, non-hierarchical organization. Its members had come to the Zicklin School of Business at Baruch College, the only MBA-granting public school in New York City, to explain how they won three Grammys this year and have become an annual fixture at Carnegie Hall without ever having an onstage boss.

It was a compelling sight: Artists who make about $30,000 a year teaching would-be executives who will bring home twice that in their first year out of school. But Orpheus has more in common with some of America's largest companies than the casual observer might think. The group has become a living, and entertaining, microcosm of a management theory that has been transforming Corporate America throughout the 1990s.

Spurred first by the corporate downsizing that began the decade and then by the Internet explosion that is ending it, hundreds of American companies are trying to become "flatter" by removing management layers between top executives and people in the field. The movement began as an effort to cut costs, but it has picked up steam, even during the current economic expansion, as executives try to reshape their companies to react quickly to technological change.

"Speed is becoming the most important criterion for growth and survival," said C. K. Prahalad, a professor at the University of Michigan Business School who has advised Citicorp and Oracle. "That is taking decision-making and accountability to levels that are closest to the business."

A 1996 survey of large companies by the Center for Effective Organizations at the University of Southern California found that 78 percent had removed at least one layer of management in the previous decade, while 14 percent reported getting rid of at least three.

The proponents of flatter structures are some of the best-performing companies of the 1990s, like Wal-Mart and Cisco Systems. "The more nodes in a communications link, the more likely it is that bad information goes up to the top," said Steven Kerr, the vice president for leadership development at General Electric, which has tried to remove management layers. At their worst, Kerr added, bureaucratic organizations can resemble the childhood game of telephone, in which children line up and pass a whispered message from one to the next, only to have the end result barely resemble the original statement.

Orpheus—named for a mythological Greek character whose beautiful music tamed wild beasts—has never needed to eliminate layers because, onstage at least, it has never had any. Julian Fifer, a cellist, and a few friends founded the group in 1972 with the aim of replicating the give-and-take of small chamber music groups in the larger setting of a chamber orchestra.

For every piece, a core group of musicians meets to decide how to play it. The first violinist, known as the concertmaster, typically leads the rehearsals, distilling the core group's plan into one voice. During pauses, other musicians call out suggestions, or objections, and hold smaller debates within their section of the orchestra.

When disagreements arise, Orpheus members try to talk them out until they reach a consensus. Failing that, they take a vote.

It is not always smooth sailing. Last year, Fifer, who had stopped playing with the group in 1990, stepped down as its executive director, a job in which he oversaw the group's schedule and business matters. His resignation came after he had clashed with group members who thought Orpheus was spending too much time on international tours.

Without a conductor to make final decisions, smaller matters can be tricky, too. At the Zicklin School rehearsal, the students noticed that some musicians had spoken much more often than others and wondered whether more outgoing people had too big a say in decisions. Many of the musicians smiled, to acknowledge that this was an issue, but said they tried to speak up frequently only when they were members of the core group.

As a whole, however, they are not shy about offering criticism. At Zicklin, for example, violinist Nardo Poy stood up at one point and said, "I know it's water music, but it sounds like it's a little at sea." At another break, Ms. Sato politely but firmly dismissed a criticism by waving her hand and saying, "We are working on this."

In a standard orchestra, where the conductor is king, such give-and-take is virtually unheard of. Much as a corporate vice president's word can be final in a highly structured company, musicians do not question a conductor during rehearsal. One result is a message that is clear but, Orpheus members say, stifles creativity.

Renee Jolles, a violinist who plays with the group frequently, said, "When you play with a conductor, it's easy to sit there and do what you're told."

Orpheus members, by contrast, are willing to lend advice to other musicians, knowing that critiquing the performance is not the job solely of one person.

"Orpheus gives every individual the opportunity to lead," said Harvey Seifter, the current executive director. "But it also creates an imperative that everyone pull together."

That seeming contradiction has helped the group land consulting gigs. Earlier this year, Kraft Foods invited Orpheus to its Illinois headquarters in an attempt to teach product managers to be more honest about their disagreements, Seifter said. And over the next two years, the orchestra will hold seminars for hospital administrators in the United States and for companies in Berlin and Paris. Eventually, Seifter said, 10 percent of the orchestra's income could come from such activities.

Companies, for their part, are hoping that shedding bureaucracy will help them replicate the connection that Orpheus members, who often devote hours to hashing out musical decisions, feel to the group. That connection can reduce employee turnover, which has become a crucial issue for businesses as the unemployment rate has fallen to its lowest level in 29 years.

Sturman Industries, a mechanical-valve designer in Woodland Park, Colorado, might be considered the Orpheus of the corporate world. The 140-person company is split into 12 functional groups, each with a coordinator who oversees administrative functions and can make final decisions when a consensus is unreachable. Other than the coordinators and the company's president, Carol Sturman, nobody has a title.

"It's not the easy route," Ms. Sturman said, because people are used to working in a more structured environment and are sometimes confused about what to do. But it has paid off: Sales at Sturman, a privately held company, are expected to increase 60 percent this year. And since moving to Colorado from California three years ago, the company said it had lost only four employees, a remarkable retention rate in the current labor market.

The move toward flatter organizations shows little sign of abating. Management textbooks, which once extolled "seven-by-seven" companies that had seven levels of management and assigned seven workers to most managers, now trumpet the elimination of hierarchy.

Business schools besides Zicklin are training their students to work in a less structured world, too. At the Wharton School at the University of Pennsylvania, for example, Professor Michael Useem has brought an improvisational acting group into his classroom and led a group of MBA's on trekking trips in the Himalayas, all with an eye to better understanding how less structured groups interact.

"When you have a hierarchical structure, you can get away with having managers who get people to do things because of their position," said Mike Jenner, who teaches leadership at the University of Chicago. The more relevant question now, he said, is "how can you manage the performance of others when you don't have the power over them?"

The New York Times, November 10, 1999
http://www.nytimes.com/library/financial/111099manage-orpheus.html

CRITICAL THINKING QUESTIONS

1. Is a "Leaderless Orchestra" a utopian ideal? Is a leaderless orchestra possible in a business or government setting? Why, or why not?
2. Won't there always be a social hierarchy? Managerial hierarchy? Even if we flatten organizations' managerial hierarchy, won't there still be a need for someone to lead? And if so, aren't we merely exchanging one system (the formal) for another (the informal)?
3. In a formal management structure, the employee has some protection (rules, regulations and procedures), but in a social hierarchy, like the Orpheus Orchestra, will these protections exist? Or will the most popular or the most powerful rule?

STORY-SPECIFIC QUESTIONS

1. The article mentions two factors spurring the trend toward a flattened organizational hierarchy. What are they?
2. What, according to Prahalad, has become the most important criterion for growth and survival in today's business world? And how does Prahalad recommend accomplishing this?
3. What is the decision-making method used by Orpheus and by Sturman Industries?
4. List two reasons why consensus is the preferred decision-making method.
5. What other problem in a flattened organization does Mike Jenner, from the University of Chicago, note?

SHORT APPLICATION ASSIGNMENTS

1. In teams or individually, answer the story-specific questions; keep your answers to 25–75 words for each question.
2. In teams of three to five persons, or as a whole class, discuss your responses to the critical thinking questions.
3. Prepare a one-page memo report (200–250 words) to your instructor in which you summarize this article. You will find a model one-page report on the Web site nytimes.swcollege.com).
4. Write an executive summary (200–250 words). As an administrative assistant to a busy executive, you are expected to summarize selected articles and present important points. You will find a model executive summary on the Web site.
5. Summarize this article (100–125 words) for your company's newsletter. You will find a model newsletter article on the Web site.

BUILDING RESEARCH SKILLS

1. The author asserts that downsizing was one of the factors prompting the flatter organization. Using at least three other references (e.g., books, research-journal articles, newspaper or magazine stories or credible Web sites), write an 800- to 1,000-word essay exploring the brief history of downsizing.
2. Using the Sturman Industries Web site (www.sturmanindustries.com/) and at least two other references (e.g., books, research-journal articles, newspaper or magazine stories or credible Web sites), investigate Sturman's management practices—specifically, how they function as a flatter organization. Your instructor may ask you to submit a three- to five-page essay, post a Web page or report your results in a five-minute presentation, along with a letter of transmittal explaining your findings.
3. Using at least two other references (e.g., books, research-journal articles, newspaper or magazine stories or credible Web sites), research how the flatter organization relates to the ideas of complexity theory discussed in Chapter 3. Your instructor may ask you to submit a three- to five-page essay, post a Web page or report your results in a five-minute presentation, along with a letter of transmittal explaining your findings.